THE SKILLS OF CAREER PLACEMENT

THE SKILLS OF CAREER PLACEMENT

PSYCHIATRIC REHABILITATION PRACTICE SERIES: book 5

Richard M. Pierce, Ph.D.
Director of Training Services
Carkhuff Institute of Human Technology
Amherst, Massachusetts

Mikal R. Cohen, Ph.D.
Director of Training, Center for Rehabilitation
   Research and Training in Mental Health
Research Associate Professor
Department of Rehabilitation Counseling
Sargent College of Allied Health Professions
Boston University

William A. Anthony, Ph.D.
Director, Center for Rehabilitation Research and
   Training in Mental Health
Associate Professor
Department of Rehabilitation Counseling
Sargent College of Allied Health Professions
Boston University

Barry F. Cohen, Ph.D.
Director of Health Care Services
Carkhuff Institute of Human Technology
Amherst, Massachusetts

Theodore W. Friel, Ph.D.
Director of Management Systems
Carkhuff Institute of Human Technology
Amherst, Massachusetts

University Park Press
Baltimore

UNIVERSITY PARK PRESS
International Publishers in Science, Medicine, and Education
233 East Redwood Street
Baltimore, Maryland 21202

This book was developed by the Carkhuff Institute of Human Technology, 22 Amherst Road, Amherst, MA 01002, pursuant to Public Health Service Grant No. T21 MH 14502-20 with the National Institute of Mental Health; Alcohol, Drug Abuse, and Mental Health Administration, Department of Health, Education and Welfare.

THE PSYCHIATRIC REHABILITATION PRACTICE SERIES

Instructor's Guide
by *William A. Anthony, Ph.D.,*
Mikal R. Cohen, Ph.D., and Richard M. Pierce, Ph.D.

Book 1: **The Skills of Diagnostic Planning** / *William A. Anthony, Richard M. Pierce, Mikal R. Cohen, and John R. Cannon*
Book 2: **The Skills of Rehabilitation Programming** / *William A. Anthony, Richard M. Pierce, Mikal R. Cohen, and John R. Cannon*
Book 3: **The Skills of Professional Evaluation** / *Mikal R. Cohen, William A. Anthony, Richard M. Pierce, Leroy A. Spaniol, and John R. Cannon*
Book 4: **The Skills of Career Counseling** / *Richard M. Pierce, Mikal R. Cohen, William A. Anthony, Barry F. Cohen, and Theodore W. Friel*
Book 5: **The Skills of Career Placement** / *Richard M. Pierce, Mikal R. Cohen, William A. Anthony, Barry F. Cohen, and Theodore W. Friel*
Book 6: **The Skills of Community Service Coordination** / *Mikal R. Cohen, Raphael L. Vitalo, William A. Anthony, and Richard M. Pierce*

Library of Congress Cataloging in Publication Data
Main entry under title:

The skills of career placement.
  (Psychiatric rehabilitation practice series; book 5)
  Bibliography: p.
  1. Mentally ill—Rehabilitation. 2. Vocational rehabilitation. I. Pierce, Richard M. II. Series.
[RC439.5.S54]   362.2'04256   79-29689
ISBN 0-8391-1577-6

THE SKILLS OF
CAREER PLACEMENT

CONTENTS

ABOUT THE AUTHORS

Dr. Richard M. Pierce is Director of Training Services at the Carkhuff Institute of Human Technology, a non-profit organization dedicated to increasing human effectiveness. Dr. Pierce has extensive counseling experience and has consulted to dozens of local, state and federal human service programs. He has taught the skills and knowledge of psychiatric rehabilitation to practitioners from a variety of disciplines. Dr. Pierce is noted for his research on the training of counselors. Dr. Pierce has authored eight books and dozens of articles in professional journals.

Dr. Mikal R. Cohen is the Director of Rehabilitation and Mental Health Services at the Carkhuff Institute of Human Technology, a non-profit organization dedicated to increasing human effectiveness. Dr. Cohen has been a practitioner in several outpatient and inpatient mental health settings, and has served as an administrator, inservice trainer, program evaluator and consultant to numerous rehabilitation and mental health programs. She has developed teaching curricula and taught the skills of psychiatric rehabilitation to practitioners throughout the United States. Furthermore, Dr. Cohen has authored a number of books and articles in the fields of mental health and health care.

Dr. William A. Anthony is an Associate Professor and Director of Clinical Training in the Department of Rehabilitation Counseling, Sargent College of Allied Health Professions, Boston University. Dr. Anthony has been Project Director of a National Institute of Mental Health grant designed to develop and evaluate training materials for persons studying and practicing in the field of Psychiatric Rehabilitation. Dr. Anthony has been involved in the field of Psychiatric Rehabilitation in several different capacities. He has researched various aspects of psychiatric rehabilitation practice and has authored over three dozen articles about psychiatric rehabilitation which have appeared in professional journals.

Dr. Barry F. Cohen is Director of Health Services Programs at the Carkhuff Institute of Human Technology. Dr. Cohen has had extensive experience in several mental health settings as an administrator, staff trainer and consultant. He has been the administrator of a community mental health center and has led faculty development workshops for health care faculty throughout the United States. Dr. Cohen has authored numerous publications in the fields of mental health and health care services.

Dr. Theodore W. Friel is Director of Management Systems at the Carkhuff Institute of Human Technology. Formerly with IBM, Dr. Friel is best known for his award-winning development of the Educational and Career Exploration System (ECES), a computer-based career guidance program which, in 1974, was hailed as "the program of the 1980's". He is currently developing management and training systems designed to increase the effectiveness of human service organizations. Dr. Friel is the author of eight books and numerous professional articles.

CARKHUFF INSTITUTE of HUMAN TECHNOLOGY

The Carkhuff Institute of Human Technology is intended to serve as a non-profit international center for the creation, development and application of human technology. The Institute, the first of its kind anywhere in the world, takes its impetus from the comprehensive human resource development models of Dr. Robert R. Carkhuff. Using these models as functional prototypes, the Institute's people synthesize human experience and objective technology in the form of a wide range of specific programs and applications.

We live in a complex technological society. Only recently have we begun to recognize and struggle with two crucially important facts: improperly used, our technology creates as many problems as it solves; and this same technology has been delivered to us with no apparent control or "off" buttons. Our attempts to retreat to some pretechnological, purely humanistic state have been both foolish and ill-fated. If we are to develop our resources and actualize our real potential, we must learn to grow in ways which integrate our scientific and applied knowledge about the human condition with the enduring human values which alone can make our growth meaningful.

We cannot afford to waste more time in fragmentary and ill-conceived endeavors. The next several decades — and perhaps far less than that — will be a critical period in our collective history. Recognizing this, the Carkhuff Institute of Human Technology is dedicated to fostering the growth and development of personnel who can develop, plan, implement and evaluate human resource development programs while making direct contributions to the scientific and technological bases of these same programs. Thus the Institute's fundamental mission is to integrate full technical potency with fully human and humane goals — in other words, to deliver skills to people which let them become effective movers and creators rather than impotent victims.

CARKHUFF INSTITUTE of HUMAN TECHNOLOGY

22 AMHERST ROAD
AMHERST, MA 01002
(413) 256-0169

PSYCHIATRIC REHABILITATION PRACTICE SERIES

PREFACE

This text is one of a series of six books designed to facilitate the teaching of various psychiatric rehabilitation skills. It is written for professionals practicing in the field as well as for students studying in such professions as nursing, rehabilitation counseling, occupational therapy, psychology, psychiatry, and social work. Each of these disciplines has contributed and will continue to contribute practitioners, researchers, administrators, and teachers to the field of psychiatric rehabilitation.

This series of training manuals evolved from a lengthy analysis of the practitioner skills that seemed to facilitate the rehabilitation outcome of persons with psychiatric disabilities. Under the sponsorship of the National Institute of Mental Health, each of these training manuals was developed and then field-tested on a group of rehabilitation mental health professionals and students. Based on the feedback of the training participants after the use of these skills with psychiatrically disabled clients, each training manual was revised. Thus, the content of the books reflects not only the authors' perspectives, but also the ideas of the initial group of training participants.

The ultimate purpose of this six-volume series is to improve the rehabilitation services that are presently offered to the psychiatrically disabled person. This training text is written for those practitioners whose rehabilitation mission is either: (1) to assist in the reintegration of the psychiatrically disabled client into the community; or (2) to maintain the ability of the formerly disabled client to continue functioning in the community and, in so doing, to prevent a reoccurrence of psychiatric disability. In other words, depending upon a client's particular situation, psychiatric rehabilitation practitioners attempt either to reduce their clients' dependence on the mental health system or maintain whatever level of independence the clients have already been able to achieve.

This mission can be accomplished when the focus of the psychiatric rehabilitation practitioner's concern is increasing the *skills* and *abilities* of the psychiatrically disabled client. More specifically, the rehabilitation practitioner works to promote the client's ability to employ those skills necessary to live, learn, and/or work in the community. Success is achieved when the client is able to function in the community as independently as possible.

Historically, the primary focus in psychiatric rehabilitation has been on the development of alternative living, learning, and working environments. In such environments, psychiatrically disabled clients have been provided settings in which they can function at a reduced level of skilled performance that is still higher than the level of functioning typically demanded in an institutional setting. In addition, these rehabilitation settings have provided a more humane, active, and "normal" environment within which clients can function. The hope has been that, over a period of time, the more positive environment of these rehabilitation settings might help many clients to improve their ability to function more independently and, in many cases, to actually leave the rehabilitation setting.

Within the last decade, however, rehabilitation has come to involve much more than the development, administration, and coordination of specific settings. Psychiatric rehabilitation practitioners can now assume a direct rehabilitation role by *diagnosing critical skill deficits* in their clients and *prescribing rehabilitation programs* designed to overcome these skill deficits. The development of rehabilitation settings that emphasize the skills and abilities of the clients has helped lay the foundation for this approach to psychiatric rehabilitation.

Although the greatest boon to rehabilitation within the mental health system has been the development of new and unique environmental settings as alternatives to institutional living, the most significant failure of psychiatric rehabilitation has been its inability to train the psychiatric rehabilitation practitioner thoroughly in rehabilitation skills. Professionals from a wide range of disciplines (e.g., counseling, nursing, psychiatry, social work, and psychology) engage in the practice of psychiatric rehabilitation. For the most part, however, these various disciplines have only the expertise developed in their own professions to bring to the field of psychiatric rehabilitation. Their training has lacked a specific set of rehabilitation skills to complement the expertise of their own disciplines.

The present series of psychiatric rehabilitation training texts, of which this volume is a part, is designed to help overcome the lack of specialized training in psychiatric rehabilitation. These training books focus on the specific skills areas that are designed to equip the psychiatric rehabilitation practitioner with the expertise necessary to promote the abilities of the psychiatrically disabled client, either by increasing the client's skills and by modifying the environment so as to better accommodate the client's present level of skilled behavior.

The first two training books help the psychiatric rehabilitation practitioner to become more proficient in *diagnosing* and *teaching* the skills that the client needs to function more effectively in the community. The third book provides the practitioner with the skills necessary to *evaluate* the outcome of her or his rehabilitative efforts. Training books four and five focus specifically on practitioner skills that have been the traditional concern of the rehabilitation practitioner — *career counseling* and *career placement* skills. The sixth training book focuses on ways in which the rehabilitation practitioner can *use the resources of the community* to better accommodate the client's present abilities and programming needs.

Although each text is part of a series of training books, each has been designed so that it may be used independently of the other. The six books included in the series are:

1. **The Skills of Diagnostic Planning**
2. **The Skills of Rehabilitation Programming**
3. **The Skills of Professional Evaluation**
4. **The Skills of Career Counseling**
5. **The Skills of Career Placement**
6. **The Skills of Community Service Coordination**

The skills-learning *process* within the training books involves an explain-demonstrate-practice format. That is, the practitioner is first explained the skill, is then shown examples of the skill, and finally is provided with suggestions on how to practice or do the skill. The practice suggestions include first practicing in a simulated situation and then actually performing the skill with a psychiatrically disabled client.

The first chapter of each training book overviews the specific practitioner skills that comprise that text. The next several chapters of each text are the teaching chapters and present the explain-demonstrate-practice steps involved in learning each specific skill. The final chapter of each book suggests ways in which the practitioner can evaluate one's own or another person's performance of these skills. The reference section of the books contains the major references that are sources of further discussion of various aspects of the skills.

Each of the major teaching chapters has a vignette at the beginning and end of the chapter. This vignette or short story is designed to illustrate unsuccessful and successful applications of the specific skills that are the focus of that particular chapter. Its purpose is to give the reader an overview of the skills that are presented in each chapter. In addition, a summary of the skill behaviors that comprise each major skill is given at the end of each chapter section.

Each chapter contains practice suggestions for each skill that can facilitate the learners' practice of their newly developing skills. Often the learner is first asked to practice and demonstrate her or his skill learning by filling out some type of table or chart. These charts can serve as an observable demonstration of the learner's mastery of a particular skill. Most of these various charts are not needed in the day-to-day application of these skills with actual clients. However, during the skill-learning process, these charts or tables are useful in demonstrating the learner's present level of skill mastery, either to the learner her or himself or to the learner's supervisors and teachers.

The skill-learning *outcome* of each of these training volumes is an observable, measurable cluster of practitioner skills. These skills are not meant to replace the skills of the various disciplines currently involved in the practice of psychiatric rehabilitation; rather, these skills are seen as complementary to the professional's existing skills. The additional use of these rehabilitation skills can play an extremely important role in improving the efficacy of psychiatric rehabilitation.

The Psychiatric Rehabilitation Practice Series has developed out of the contributions of a number of different people. We are particularly indebted to a great many students and practicing professionals, who, by virtue of their willingness to learn these skills and provide knowledge as to their effectiveness, have allowed us the opportunity to develop, refine, and revise these texts.

We would also like to acknowledge the individual instructors who taught the first group of students from these texts, and gave willingly of their time and talents in the development of this series.

These initial instructors were Arthur Dell Orto, Marianne Farkas, Robert Lasky, Patrice Muchowske, Paul Power, Don Shrey and LeRoy Spaniol.

Particular appreciation is expressed to Marianne Farkas, who not only taught these skills, but who also assisted in the editing and evaluation of these training texts.

Boston, Massachusetts   W.A.A.
                                                        M.R.C.
                                                        R.M.P.

THE SKILLS OF CAREER PLACEMENT

Chapter 1 THE CAREER PLACEMENT MODEL

Stated most broadly, the goal of psychiatric rehabilitation is to restore to clients their capacity to function in the community. Philosophically, this means that rehabilitation is directed at increasing the *strengths* of the clients so that they can achieve their maximum potential for independent living and meaningful careers. Although many traditional treatment approaches seek to prepare clients to function independently, the emphasis in traditional psychiatric treatment has typically been on the reduction of client discomfort by changing underlying personality structures, increasing client insights, and alleviating symptomatology.

Although the total treatment process for disabled psychiatric clients includes both aspects of traditional psychiatric treatment and psychiatric therapy and rehabilitation, it is important that these activities be separated conceptually so that the rehabilitation process receives the emphasis necessary to develop its own unique contribution to client care.

This text represents one of a series of books whose purpose is to define and teach the unique skills of psychiatric rehabilitation. The particular skill with which this book is concerned is that of *career placement*.

THE DEFINITION, PURPOSE, AND APPLICATIONS OF CAREER PLACEMENT

WHAT CAREER PLACEMENT IS

Career placement refers to the process by which the rehabilitation practitioner helps the client to acquire the best vocational position. More specifically, this means helping clients to identify their qualifications, to find where these qualifications can be used, and then to effectively present these qualifications both in person and in writing. Simply stated, the practitioner helps clients to understand *what* they have to offer, *where* to offer it, and *how* to offer it.

WHY CAREER PLACEMENT IS IMPORTANT

The purpose of career placement is to equip clients with the skills and knowledge they need to compete effectively for a vocational position. Unfortunately, the problems and complications involved in rehabilitating the psychiatrically disabled client into a work environment are immense (Anthony, 1979). For example, consider these facts:

1. Successful adjustment to a living or learning environment does not correlate significantly with adjustment to a work environment.

2. Clients often lose their jobs, not because of an inability to perform job tasks but because of skill deficits in the emotional-interpersonal area of functioning.

3. Clients who do lose their jobs often do not possess the skills necessary to obtain new jobs. Consequently, they do not try to find employment and often return to the rehabilitation practitioner for further help.

4. There is no relationship between hospital-based work therapy and competitive employment. The work behavior of the psychiatrically disabled client is situation-specific.

5. Previous studies of employment success rates show that approximately 30–50 percent of discharged patients obtain employment but that less than 25 percent maintain full-time employment (Anthony, Buell, Sharratt, and Atthoff, 1972). With an increasing number of long-term patients being discharged from the hospital, the current full-time employment percentages may be considerably less (Anthony, Cohen, and Vitalo, 1978).

Because of these problems, increased attention has been directed to the process of career placement and the preparation of practitioners skilled in the practice of career placement. Basically, there are several reasons why it is important for rehabilitation practitioners to be able to improve clients' career placement skills. First, clients who possess placement skills are more likely to obtain their desired placements, for reasons both qualitative and quantitative. Quantitatively, the clients would be able to generate more application opportunities. Qualitatively, they would be able to present themselves in a better light to interviewers or other placement decision makers.

There is not a significant number of studies concerning the effectiveness of teaching career placement skills to clients (Zadny and James, 1976), but existing data support the notion that clients can, in fact, be trained to improve their career placement abilities (Keil and Barber, 1973; Prazak, 1969; Safieri, 1970). Most importantly, these skills do seem to have significant impact on various measures of employment outcome (Anderson, 1968; Keith, Engelkes, and Winborn, 1977; McClure, 1973; Pumo, Sehl, and Cogan, 1966). Psychiatrically disabled clients frequently have difficulty not only in obtaining jobs but also in holding jobs. The more skilled clients are in placement activities, the better the chances are that they can obtain the type of position they will be motivated to retain. This is partially due to the fact that clients who are skilled in career placement will have more and better opportunities for job placement. In addition, such clients are less likely to just "up and leave," because they have developed an investment in job position by having actively participated in the job-seeking process. Finally, when clients want or need to change jobs, they have a better chance of obtaining new employment, and without the renewed services of the rehabilitation practitioner. In essence, career placement skills are important because they contribute to both the acquisition and the retention of positions by the psychiatrically disabled client.

WHEN CAREER PLACEMENT CAN BE USED

Career placement is appropriate for any psychiatrically disabled client who is diagnosed as having deficiencies in the career placement areas. The following are common client deficits in the placement area:

I.   **Inability to identify assets:** The client is unable to articulate factually based assets that would make him/her attractive for a potential position.

   A.   The client cannot articulate factual evidence indicative of his/her *ability to perform the tasks* required by the position.

   B.   The client cannot articulate factual evidence indicative of his/her *dependability* (e.g., attendance, punctuality).

   C.   The client cannot articulate factual evidence indicative of his/her *ability to relate to other people* (e.g., getting along with peers and supervisors, supervising others).

II.   **Inability to develop potential job positions:** The client is unable to identify a sufficient number of sources where she/he could obtain the type of position desired.

   A.   The client cannot list *general types of places* where she/he might secure the desired position.

   B.   The client cannot list *specific places* where she/he might secure the desired position.

III.   **Inability to present self in writing:** The client is unable to present him/herself in a manner that would facilitate obtaining the desired position.

   A.   The client cannot fill out the necessary *application forms*.

   B.   The client cannot write a *cover letter or a resume* that would effectively present his/her assets.

IV.   **Inability to present self in person:** The client is unable to present her/himself in an interview in a manner that would facilitate acquiring the desired position.

3

A. The client lacks the *interpersonal skills* for the interview situation.
B. The client lacks the *ability to answer* the interviewer's questions.
C. The client lacks the *ability to ask* the interviewer appropriate questions.
D. The client lacks the *ability to review* the interview to determine her/his status.

A client may have some or all of the placement deficits outlined above. For example, one client may be able to fill out an application form but may not possess the interpersonal skills necessary for the interview. In other instances, the client may not need all the placement skills because his/her unique situation simply does not require them. For example, a client may not be able to identify any potential employers but knows that the State Employment Service has a record of all job openings in the area. Or a client may not need to be able to write a cover letter because the rehabilitation practitioner may have already made the contact for the client.

In all of the cases cited above, the practitioner would need to work with the client to overcome only those deficits unique to the client and relevant to the desired position. Thus, although a particular client may not need all the placement skills, the practitioner should possess all the skills; such a highly skilled practitioner would have a repertoire that would enable her/him to meet the placement needs of any individual case.

Placement strategies are appropriate skills to master for anyone who is working or planning to work with older adolescent or adult psychiatrically disabled clients in order to assist them in working more independently. The clients may be inpatients or outpatients; they may be preparing for placement in a competitive or a sheltered environment. In the latter case, the clients' mastery of the placement skills will usually be viewed as preparation for later, competitive placements.

The practitioner can work with clients to develop opportunities for placement in either individual or group contexts. The number of clients will depend upon the amount of individual attention the individuals require in order to be able to complete the needed tasks. It should also be noted that career placement skills can be introduced at any point in the rehabilitation treatment process. That is, placement opportunities can be developed with clients prior to the rehabilitation program, concurrent with the program, or after the program has been completed. The determining criterion is the point at which it is appropriate for clients to participate in the development of their own career placement opportunities.

The practitioner typically arrives at the diagnosis of the specific client career placement deficits in one of two ways. If the client has been referred to the practitioner specifically for career placement concerns, the practitioner can facilitate the diagnosis by using the checklist presented in the last chapter of this book (Table 24). The practitioner can then use those career placement skills that will best meet the client's career placement needs. In other cases, the diagnosis may occur during the more comprehensive diagnostic planning process (see Book 1 in this series). The diagnostic planning process assesses client skill behaviors in living, learning, and working environments. Many of the diagnosed client deficits that affect client functioning in a working environment can then be given attention by using either the career placement skills of this book or the career counseling skills outlined in Book 4 of this series.

THE STAGES AND SKILLS OF CAREER PLACEMENT

This book focuses on how career placement is accomplished. This section will give a brief overview of the process. As indicated previously, the goal of career placement is to enable the client to attain the desired vocational position. In order to achieve this goal, three major steps need to be covered. These steps are developmental in nature. That is, the clients need to identify *what* they have to offer before looking for a place in which to offer it. Similarly, clients need to know *where* to offer something before they can learn *how* to apply for the job itself.

Thus, in most cases the clients proceed by initially *exploring* their past work and educational experiences in order to identify the assets they have to offer an employer. Once this exploratory process has been completed, the clients work to *understand* the specific businesses, agencies, or institutions where their assets may be appropriately offered. Finally, clients *act* to offer their assets, both in writing and in person. Table 1 presents an outline of these stages and skills of career placement.

Clients can achieve the maximal amount of independence if they not only complete each of the major steps but also learn *how* to do each of the steps themselves. Obviously, the amount of learning the client achieves will vary according to the client's level of functioning. Yet, even low-level functioning clients, who cannot learn how to perform many of the career placement skills without the continued assistance of the rehabilitation practitioner, can be helped by the career placement process. The observable, step-by-step nature of the career placement process can serve to maximize client understanding and involvement in career placement activities. As a general principle, however, the practitioner can work with the clients to help them to actually learn the career placement process, so that they will be able to replicate the placement process at a future point, independent of the practitioner.

In order to move a client through the three phases of career placement, the practitioner needs two sets of skills: (1) placement skills and

Table 1. The Stages and Skills of Career Placement

I. *EXPLORE ASSETS*

   A. Explore work and educational experience

   B. Identify assets from work and educational experience

II. *UNDERSTAND WORK OPPORTUNITIES*

   A. Determine geographical limits

   B. Identify advertised job openings

   C. Identify unadvertised job openings

III. *ACT TO GET A JOB*

   A. Present self in writing

   B. Present self in person

(2) structured interviewing skills. Initially, the practitioner needs to master the content of career placement, and this, of course, is the focus of this book. A variety of interviewing skills have been discussed in detail in Book 1 in this series, and that discussion will not be repeated here. Suffice it to say that, in order to maximize the benefits of a structured interview situation, the practitioner will want to have a minimum of three interviewing skills: (1) responding to content, (2) responding to feeling, and (3) responding to feeling and content.

Responding to content involves being able to accurately summarize the client's verbal expressions. A format that can be used is, *"You're saying _____,"* or, *"In other words, _____"*. For example:

Client Statement:	*Gee, I've gone through the data processing training, but now I can't find a job. I've really tried, but I just can't find anything. The employers ask why I haven't been employed for the last eight months, and when I tell them, it's over.*
Practitioner Response to Content:	*You're saying that no one will give you a real chance at a job.*

In a **response to feeling,** the practitioner responds to the client's feelings about the content. A format to use is, *"You feel _____."* Thus, to the above, the practitioner might respond as follows: *"You feel discouraged."*

The third interviewing skill involves practitioner **response to both feeling and content.** The format here is, *"You feel _____ because _____."* In response to the earlier client statement, the practitioner might say: *"You feel discouraged because no one will give you a real chance at a job."*

These types of responses serve two purposes. First, they enable the practitioner to ascertain if she/he really understands the situation. Second, research studies have shown that these types of responses encourage the client to discuss the problem further (Cannon and Pierce, 1968; Truax and Carkhuff, 1967). Whether the practitioner responds to content, feeling, or both will depend upon whether she/he wants the client to talk more about the content, the feeling, or both.

In summary, then, to take the client through the three phases of career placement, the practitioner will need both the structured interviewing skills cited above and the career placement skills presented in this manual. It would also be valuable for the practitioner to become familiar with some of the issues in the career placement field (e.g., Levitan and Taggert, 1977; Zadny and James, 1976).

In addition, the placement process can be made more efficient if, before the placement process has begun, the client has decided upon a specific and realistic position in which to obtain placement. The practitioner skills of career counseling, discussed in detail in Book 4, *The Skills of Career Counseling,* enable the client to identify a specific career objective. Although a decision may be based on the exploration of experience and competency (i.e., the client goes after the best job for which she/he is qualified), in many cases it will be wise to go through a more detailed career planning process. The client should begin the placement process with a specific goal in mind.

The remainder of this book will focus on the career placement skills that will help the practitioner to assist clients in obtaining their career objectives. The book will address the application of the placement skills to both employment and educational environments. However, because the majority of psychiatrically disabled clients are primarily interested in employment rather than placement in highly competitive training or educational programs, the book will first focus on job placement, including on-the-job training. Chapter 5 will deal with the application of these skills to obtaining a position in a competitive school or training program.

Chapter 2 EXPLORING THE CLIENT'S ASSETS

EXPLORING ASSETS: AN UNSKILLED APPROACH

"Hey, what about this one?" Peter leaned over Sue's shoulder, his finger pointing to an ad about halfway down the skimpy "Help Wanted" column in the newspaper.

Opening for salesperson in women's fashions. Large department store seeks experienced clerk. Advancement opportunity for right person. Applications at Personnel Office, Bartolo's.

Sue nodded, slowly at first and then vigorously as she finished reading.

"Gee, it sounds just right for me," she said. There was a wistful note in her voice as she added, "I wonder if I'd really have a chance ..."

"Why not?" Peter tried to put as much confidence as he could in his voice. "After all, didn't you tell me you'd worked in a department store somewhere before? Well, that's experience, right? And it says right there that they're looking for an experienced person!"

Sue nodded again. "Uh-huh. Only — only when I worked before, that was — you know — before I got all messed up."

Peter sat down behind his desk, making a conscious effort to smile at her. "Listen, don't worry about all of that. You're experienced. And you want the job. Nothing else really matters, does it?"

His enthusiasm was contagious. Sue's face relaxed into a smile. "You make it sound easy," she said. "Maybe you're right. It sure would be great to get back to work!"

"Of course it would be. And of course I'm right. You just make sure you get down there before five this afternoon and fill out one of those applications. And let me know how you make out, OK?"

Sue didn't need any further encouragement. She caught a bus outside the clinic that dropped her off right down the street from Bartolo's. All she could think of was how perfect it would be if she got the job. It sounded just right for her: a job that she knew she could handle, an ideal way to start putting her life back together again. And why shouldn't she get the job? After all, she was experienced, right?

The personnel office consisted of a large outer room with a receptionist and several long tables with chairs along one wall. The receptionist provided Sue with an application form and told her that a Mrs. Wesson would see her as soon as she had completed the application. Sue could see an older woman — presumably Mrs. Wesson — holding forth behind a desk in a smaller side office; she was listening to someone — presumably another applicant — who was sitting out of Sue's line of sight.

It was almost five, and the outer office was empty except for the receptionist. Sue tried not to think about the other people who might be competing for the job, tried instead to focus her attention on the application. She felt a twinge of satisfaction as she wrote, "One year as clerk," after the question, "Do you have any previous sales experience?"

Sue didn't see the other person leave. One minute she was handing her application to the receptionist, and the next she was being ushered into Mrs. Wesson's smiling presence.

"Hello, Sue," the older woman greeted her, picking the name off the application with a practiced glance. Sue smiled nervously and mumbled a response. Mrs. Wesson seemed friendly enough. Maybe this wouldn't be too bad.

But it was. Having read Sue's application quickly yet thoroughly, Mrs. Wesson launched almost immediately into an apologetic explanation.

"I wish I could be more encouraging," she said. "But, you see, you've only indicated a single year of experience. Several of the other applicants have had more experience than that. So unless there's something special about your background or qualifications . . .?" Sue could only shake her head, looking away so that she didn't have to meet the other woman's politely sympathetic gaze.

"There's nothing special about me," she thought. "If only there was!"

This chapter focuses upon the inability of clients to identify the concrete assets they have to offer a potential employer. If clients know what they have to offer an employer, their chances of obtaining the desired position are increased.

The primary concern of employers in the competitive sphere is profits: assets and liabilities, accounts receivable and accounts payable, income and outgo. The phrasing does not matter. Every competitive employer makes decisions based on expected financial profits or losses. Employers in the private sector must operate at a profit if they want to stay in business. Nonprofit organizations must still operate within the strict limitations of the funds available to them.

This state of affairs has direct import for the client's application. The client needs to be able to show an employer on paper that he/she would be a valuable addition to the organization; in other words, the client's application must contain information that presents the client as a potential source of *profit*, rather than as a financial risk. Clients who can convince employers of their real value — who can show employers that they can *produce* enough to "pay their own way" — will increase their chances of obtaining an interview.

As indicated, employers' general concerns tend to focus on each applicant's status as a potential asset or a financial risk. In order to deal with this general concern, most employers ask themselves *three specific questions* about every job applicant: (1) Can this applicant *do the job?* (2) Is this applicant *dependable?* (3) Does this applicant *get along with others?* Many psychiatrically disabled clients who apply for jobs are unaware of these three separate and extremely important questions. Consequently, they fail to answer all three adequately. At worst, such clients communicate to the employer that they "need a break" and that the employer should give it to them. At best, they tell employers all about their job skills but indicate nothing about their proven dependability; or they indicate that they are dependable but fail to show the employers that they can work effectively with other people.

In addition, clients often find it difficult to speak about their assets. As individuals in a psychiatric setting, their previous exploration has often concentrated on their symptoms, their illnesses, and their problems. They may have forgotten that they do in fact have assets! Other clients may have accepted the stigma of being "mental patients" and ignored the fact that they are much more than what is represented by a label. For these clients, the asset exploration process can be a positive and enlightening experience.

The practitioner's initial career placement goal, then, will be to help clients identify the concrete facts from the past that are indicative of their ability to perform the job tasks, to be dependable, and to get along effectively with others. In order to accomplish this task, the practitioner will take the clients through several steps. First, the clients' employment history will be explored. Second, the clients will review each relevant work experience for indicators of their ability to perform the desired job, to be dependable, and to effectively relate to others. The third step will repeat the above process for the clients' relevant educational experience.

EXPLORING WORK AND EDUCATIONAL EXPERIENCE

SUMMARIZING PAST WORK EXPERIENCE

Summarizing the client's past work experience has two significant purposes. First, it serves to inform the practitioner about the types of employment the client has had. Second, the summary serves as a stimulus for the client to recall the details and responsibilities of particular jobs. Through this summarization, the client's assets and abilities will be identified.

As a first step in developing the work summary, the practitioner can help the client to develop a list of jobs held in the past. It is easiest to begin with the most recent job and work backward. Some clients may have worked only in a workshop setting that involves training and evaluation. These are often three-to-six-month positions that the clients may erroneously dismiss as legitimate experiences. Working in a hospital program as a coffee-shop attendant or typist-trainee can, however, be considered work experience.

After listing each job, the client can also list the employer and the length of time the job was held. In this regard, it is important to remember that the client may well have had more than one job with the same employer. In most cases, a five-year employment history contains sufficient information to later identify client assets. To ensure that all important jobs have been covered, the practitioner may also ask the client to add to the list any other past job that might be relevant to her/his future plans (e.g., the client would consider working at a similar job in the future). A sample work history is presented in Table 2. The job list is that of a young woman named Mary Jones. She has recently been discharged from the hospital but is continuing to work with a rehabilitation practitioner, Rufus Williams, on an outpatient basis. She wants to return to work as a clerk-typist.

Table 2. Mary's Job History

Job Title	Employer	Dates
Clerk-typist	Bradley Insurance Co.	2/73–3/74
Keypunch operator	Bradley Insurance Co.	4/72–2/73
Waitress	King's Table	6/71–4/72
Clothing sales clerk	Harrod's Dept. Store	11/70–6/71

The next step is for the client to check off all those jobs that are relevant to his/her future. As suggested above, a past job is relevant to the future if it helped in some way to qualify the client for a desired job. Once this check-off has been completed, the practitioner can help to rank the jobs from most relevant (1) to least relevant (see Table 3). If the client has no directly related work experience but would still qualify for the job, then the most relevant job would be the one at which the client was most successful as an employee.

Table 3. Mary's Job History Ranked by Relevance to Desired Job

Rank	Job Title	Employer	Dates
1	Clerk-typist	Bradley Insurance Co.	2/73–3/74
2	Keypunch operator	Bradley Insurance Co.	4/72–2/73
	Waitress	King's Table	6/71–4/72
	Clothing sales clerk	Harrod's Dept. Store	11/70–6/71

The third step is to fill out the details of each relevant job. The details can include the following information: (1) the employer for whom the client worked, (2) the length of time employed at the job, and (3) the major duties and responsibilities. These duties and responsibilities should be specifically identified. For example, a statement such as "I took care of customers in the clothing department" is vague; but a statement such as "I helped customers find what they wanted, measured them for minor fittings, handled mail and telephone orders, kept records of all sales, and maintained a running inventory of all departmental stock" is specific. The practitioner can help the client to develop a specific statement by asking, "What else did you do?" or "What kinds of things went into doing _____?" The latter is most helpful when the client's initial statement is vague. It is important that appropriate "informal" duties also be included, such as the client's informal supervision of the work of others. Often the client will be surprised to learn that what might initially seem like a rather routine job (e.g., sales clerk in a clothing department) is composed of some major tasks and responsibilities. This exploration of previous experience, even for clients with limited job histories, can indirectly serve to improve the client's feelings about her/himself. Table 4 contains a work summary statement developed by Rufus and Mary for her most relevant job experience.

Table 4. Summary of Mary's Most Relevant Work Experience

Job Title:	Clerk-typist
Employer:	Bradley Insurance Co.
Length of employment:	13 months
Details of work done:	Typed forms, letters, and reports. Did filing of office documents. Sorted mail and answered phone.

Note: Mary and Rufus developed a separate work summary for her other relevant job as a keypunch operator.

Practice Situations

As an initial practice experience, develop a work summary for a job you yourself have held that is most relevant to the type of job you might want in the future. Include the job title, employer(s), and the length of time you worked at the job. You can use a format similar to Table 5. When you have completed the exercise, continue to practice by developing a work summary with a client or a friend. As indicated previously, clients will want to learn the placement skills whenever possible so that they can be more independent in the future. Therefore, it is important that you *overview* what is involved in the process. That is, tell the client the steps you will be going through to develop the summary (i.e., list past jobs, rank the relevant jobs, develop details of duties and responsibilities) and the purpose of the summary (i.e., to collect the information from which the job assets are developed). It is best to do the overview in writing so that the client will have a better chance to learn and remember what was done. As you come to each step, give an example for each and explain any special things to think about so that the client can do the step correctly. For example, in the duties-and-responsibilities section, remind the client to be specific and explain what questions will ensure specificity.

In addition, remember to *respond* to the material the client presents to you. You can respond to content ("You're saying _____"), feeling ("You feel _____"), or both ("You feel _____ because _____"). This will help the client to know that you understand what is presented and will encourage her/him to discuss relevant material with you.

Table 5. Practice Exercise in Developing a Work Summary

Job title: _____

Employer(s): _____
_____
_____
_____

Time employed: _____

Specific duties and responsibilities: _____
_____
_____
_____
_____

Summarizing Past Work Experience: A Summary

Goal: To identify the client's assets and abilities by learning about the types of employment that the client has had and stimulating the client to recall the specific details of each job.

1. Overview with the client the steps involved in developing a summary.

2. Help the client to develop a list of each job held in the past, including the employer and the length of time the job was held.

3. Have the client check off the jobs that are relevant to his/her future (i.e., desired job).

4. Help the client to rank the jobs from most relevant to least relevant.

5. Assist the client in filling out the details of each relevant job, ensuring that these details are specific rather than vague.

6. Respond to the material presented by the client by responding to the client's feeling, content, or both.

SUMMARIZING PAST EDUCATIONAL EXPERIENCE

Like the work-experience summary, the purpose of the educational-experience summary is (1) to inform the practitioner about the client's educational history and (2) to assist the client in recalling exactly what was done and what was accomplished. Once again, this information will eventually be used to develop client assets.

As a general rule, the practitioner need work with clients to summarize only their most recent educational experiences. There are two major exceptions to this general rule. First, the client may indicate that an earlier experience is more relevant to the career goal than the most recent experience. For example, John had fourteen months of training in electronics while in the service. Upon leaving the service, he went to work as a salesman for a large department store. During this period, he took a number of business courses at the local community college in hopes of moving into a management position. Partially as a result of his psychiatric problems, he decided to get away from the pressures of management and returned to work as an electronics technician. Thus, his earlier training in the service became more relevant than his later management training.

A second exception occurs when the client's most recent training has been very brief. Here, an earlier experience can definitely add something to the client's qualifications. For example, Sam's goal was to be a long-distance truck driver, and he had attended a school to learn the required skills. However, during his high school years, he had majored in auto mechanics. Since this would add to his qualifications, he

15

Table 6. Summary of Harry's Most Relevant Educational Experience

Relevant education experience:

Graduated from Monroe Technical and Vocational High School.

Summary of all courses: check (✓) job-related courses

English I, II, III   ✓ Auto Repair Shop I–IV
✓ Business Communications I   Typing I
✓ Business Math I, II   Civics I
Basic Science I
Algebra I

Specific details of job-related courses:

Name: Auto Repair Shop I–IV.

Learned principles of internal combustion and rotary engines; mastered basic skills of diagnosing and repairing auto engines; handled problems involving carburetion, rings, cylinders, heads, distributors, transmission, and drive train. Can now deal with any repair situation from minor tune-up to engine removal and replacement. Also learned basic skills involved in trouble-shooting and fixing electrical systems.

Name: Business Communications I.

Learned how to write business letters, invoices, reports, and so on.

Name: Business Math I, II.

Learned how to use math in business situations. This included work on math problems involving auto repair situations.

---

would need to summarize both training experiences. In the end, then, the client should summarize each educational experience that adds to his/her qualifications for the desired position.

As a first step, the practitioner will want to explore with the client the educational or training experiences that are relevant to the career goal. Where the client lacks a definite career goal, the most complete formal schooling experience should be summarized (e.g., high school), as well as any special training the client has undertaken (e.g., a six-week adult education course in accounting).

To summarize an educational experience, first list all the courses that the client has completed. Then, check off those courses that are relevant to the desired objective. Finally, detail what the client learned in each of the relevant courses. As before, these details should be specific ("learned how to write business letters and invoices" rather than the vague "learned business communication procedures"). For example, Harry is a young veteran being seen in a local outpatient clinic because of "anxiety attacks." His high school experience is his most relevant educational experience. The summary of this experience, which he developed with the help of rehabilitation practitioner Carla Sanchez, appears in Table 6.

Practice Situations

Using Table 6 as a guideline, practice your educational summary skills by first summarizing your own most relevant educational experience. Use a format similar to Table 7. Once you have completed this exercise, continue to practice your skill by working with a friend or client to develop his/her educational summary. Remember to overview the steps (i.e., list courses, check off those that are relevant, and develop details), as well as to respond to the input you receive.

Table 7. Practice Exercise in Summarizing an Educational Experience

Relevant education experience:
_____

_____

Summary of all courses: check (✓) job-related courses

_____   _____
_____   _____
_____   _____
_____   _____
_____   _____

Specific details of job-related courses:
Name: _____
_____
_____

Name: _____
_____
_____

Name: _____
_____
_____

Name: _____
_____
_____

SUMMARIZING THE PAST EDUCATIONAL EXPERIENCE: A SUMMARY

Goal: To identify the client's assets and abilities by learning about the client's educational history and assisting the client in recalling experiences and accomplishments.

1. Overview with the client the steps involved in the process.

2. Explore with the client the educational or training experiences that are relevant to the career goal.

3. Summarize each educational experience that adds to the client's qualifications for the desired position by helping the client to *(a)* list all the courses completed; *(b)* check off the courses that are relevant to the desired objective; and *(c)* detail what was learned in each of the relevant courses.

4. Respond to the information presented by the client.

5. As a general rule, summarize only the client's most recent educational experience.

IDENTIFYING ASSETS FROM WORK AND EDUCATIONAL EXPERIENCE

Once the practitioner and the client have summarized the specific and relevant details of the client's work and educational history, they have collected the information from which they can identify the client's assets. The first part of this section draws on information developed from the exploration of the client's work experience. The next part is based on information obtained during the exploration of the client's educational history.

In attempting to identify the assets from work experience, the practitioner and the client seek to identify concrete facts that indicate the client's ability to (1) perform the job, (2) function as a dependable employee, and (3) relate effectively to people in the work environment. These three areas are critical concerns of almost every employer. The client will seek to show a prospective employer that he/she does indeed possess these important assets. A particular client will not necessarily have assets in all three areas, but virtually all clients have one or more assets that would be attractive to an employer. Often, the practitioner will need to assiduously explore the client's experience to identify such assets.

Each asset should be identified in terms that are as concrete and factual as possible. Concrete facts are facts that can be stated in *numbers* ("I missed only three days of work last year"), *percentages* ("I missed fewer days of work than 90 percent of my coworkers" or "I sorted mail with 95 percent accuracy in fifteen minutes less than the allocated time"), *absolute words* ("I never had an argument with my boss," "I was always on time"), and specific *amounts* ("By working out a new soap/water mixture, I saved the company over one thousand dollars annually in cleaning materials").

In order to develop a set of convincing facts, the client and the practitioner can use variations of *three basic questions.*

1. *Quantitative:* How much or how many did the client do/make/handle here?

2. *Qualitative:* How well did the client do in this area?

3. *Comparative:* How did the client's quantitative or qualitative performance compare with that of her/his peers?

Although all three of these quantitative, qualitative, and comparative questions may be used, they are not always equally helpful. The practitioner and client will want to use only questions that yield answers that present the client in the best light. For example, the client may have received four separate raises during two years of employment, but almost all coworkers may have received the same raises. Therefore, the client will want to mention the four raises in pay but will not want to compare him/herself to the coworkers, since this would present the client as only an average employee. The remainder of this section will show how these questions can generate concrete and factual assets from the client's past work and educational experience. Some of these assets will eventually be used in the client's cover letter, résumé, or preparation for the job interview. Their purpose is to communicate to the prospective employer that the client (1) can do the job, (2) is dependable, and (3) can get along with others.

Each of these three asset areas contains four subareas, which can be explored with the client, the purpose being to stimulate client and practitioner to think of the client's factual assets in an extremely comprehensive manner. The eventual goal is to uncover as many assets as possible.

It is important to note, however, that at this stage of the career placement process, practitioner and client are attempting to be as creative and expansive as possible in identifying assets. It may be that some of the assets they develop will not be used in either the cover letter, the résumé, or the job interview. However, the goal at this stage is to think of as many assets as possible. In a later phase of the career placement process, the client and the practitioner will select which of the identified assets they will actually utilize.

Table 11 provides an overview of the three asset areas and their specific subareas. The next two parts of this section will describe and give examples of each of these subareas. A practitioner skilled in career placement should be able to help the client to explore each of these subareas. It is also important to note that the process of identifying client assets serves a purpose other than that of preparing the client for later

19

stages of the career placement process. It helps to change the mind-set of some clients from a preoccupation with deficits and symptoms to a recognition of their previously ignored strengths and assets. It uncovers positive attributes that the client may have either forgotten or never recognized. The completed identification of assets will describe the client in "nonclient" terminology. Asset identification pushes the "client" characteristics into the background. It will not only make the client look better on paper but will also improve the client's self-image.

IDENTIFYING ASSETS FROM WORK EXPERIENCE

Proving That the Client Can Do the Job

In the general asset area of proving that the client can do the job, there are four subareas for the practitioner to explore with the client: (1) productivity, (2) recognition, (3) efficiency and accuracy, and (4) speed of learning.

Productivity: Every job involves some sort of production. A factory worker produces by assembling units of some kind. A gas station attendant produces by servicing customers' cars. A sheltered workshop employee produces by, for example, packing poker chips. A salesperson produces by selling merchandise. A secretary produces by typing pages. A lawyer produces by handling clients' cases. Production level on a single job may be measured in several ways. For example, a counselor may measure production in terms of the number of clients handled, the number of client contact hours, or even the number of clients who reach certain criteria set by the counselor (e.g., the number who reach their rehabilitation objectives).

The first step, then, is for the practitioner and the client to develop a method of measuring the client's production on the previous job. The second step is to ask the quantitative and qualitative questions, following each with the comparative question.

Myra worked as a salesperson in a large discount drug store. Using the information identified during the work exploration process, she decided that her job involved two different areas of "production": (1) waiting on customers, and (2) maintaining adequate displays of stock. Myra starts with the former area. She explores: *"How many people did I wait on?"* To the best of her ability, Myra recalls that she handled about ten customers during each hour of an average day — or eighty customers for each full day. Now she asks: *"How did this compare with the number waited on by my coworkers?"* Her coworkers handled about the same number. This is not helpful information because it does not "show off" Myra's abilities. *"How well did I perform?"* Myra had no complaints in the entire year she worked there. *"How did my performance compare with that of my coworkers?"* Myra's coworkers tended to be absentminded. Myra is able to recall five separate customers who complained about each of these coworkers. *"During the year that I waited on customers, I received no complaints, although my coworkers received several."* Now she has a choice. She can state this asset in absolute terms *("I never received a complaint about my work")* or in comparative terms. She decides that the comparative statement might make her sound too critical to prospective employers and decides to go with the absolute statement. It should be noted that the development and use of comparative statements may pose unique problems for practitioners as well as clients. Sometimes, the statements that are developed are too overbearing and reflect a feeling of conceit or superiority. The practitioner will want to guard against the client giving this impression. Statements that imply comparisons but focus on concrete facts seem to be the most effective — for example, "I received the highest number of commissions on sales"; or, "The average number of rooms cleaned was twenty-three, but I was able to clean twenty-five rooms."

Now Myra evaluates her production in the second area by asking herself: *"How many times did I check the levels of stock on display?"* She remembers that she used to do this three times each day, as regularly as clockwork. *"How did this compare with what my coworkers did?"* None of Myra's coworkers seemed to check the stock in their sections regularly. Still, Myra can't give their production any quantitative value so she can't compare it with her own production. She must explore further. *"How well did I perform?"* Here the answer is clear: Myra never had a customer ask for an item that was in stock but not on display. *"How did my performance compare with that of my coworkers?"* Customers always seemed to be asking Myra's coworkers why something wasn't displayed. So Myra can truthfully say: *"I was the only clerk whose section was always fully stocked with display items."*

By asking and answering appropriate questions about *both* of her production areas, Myra is able to develop some specific and comparative information.

Another example might be a workshop client who develops the following statements about her workshop productivity: *"I completed all tasks required in less than the allotted time and almost always before my coworkers. I learned the inventory-checking task, the consignment-sorting task, and the cashier-position tasks within the first month at the Thrift Shop."*

Recognition. On-the-job recognition can be either formal or informal. *Formal recognition* refers to raises in pay and specific promotions. *Informal recognition* refers to definite compliments from employers or customers. The client will want to explore the type of recognition he/she received on the job.

Juan, who worked as a custodian, asks: *"How many raises or promotions did I get?"* He received no promotions but did get four raises in the year and a half he worked for the firm. *"How did this compare with what my coworkers got?"* Juan worked with seven other people. Each of them received only three raises during the same period of time. So Juan can say: *"I received an extra raise in pay, which was given to none of my coworkers."* Now Juan asks: *"How good were my raises?"* All employees received the same twenty-five-cents-per-hour raise. Thus, despite the fact that Juan's individual raises and those given his coworkers were for the same amount, Juan now has the option of saying: *"During the year and a half I was with the agency, my pay was raised by a dollar an hour."* (Note: Juan refrains from mentioning his top pay in specific terms; he doesn't want to prejudice a prospective employer who might otherwise be willing to start him out at higher pay.)

Rita received no raises or promotions, since she was with her previous employer for only five months. She can say, however, that she received *"frequent compliments from my employer on the accuracy of my typing."* (In other words, she has asked: *"How many compliments did I get?"* and *"How did this compare with my coworkers?"* And she has found that, although she did not receive more compliments than her coworkers, she can still describe the number she received as "frequent.")

Efficiency and Accuracy. Employers are always interested in an applicant's on-the-job efficiency and accuracy — especially if they are presented in terms of potential financial savings.

Stanley worked in a "quick copy" duplicating shop. He was able to say: *"I wasted 15 percent less paper than any of my coworkers, saving my employer over ten dollars each week."* (He has asked: *"How much paper did I use?"* and *"How did this compare with what my coworkers used?"*)

Nancy's careful accuracy as an assistant in a photo-developing lab helped her to save her employer money, too. She has asked: *"How well did I develop my films?"* and *"How did this compare with my coworkers?"* Her answers allow her to say: *"I made 25 percent fewer errors in developing materials than my coworkers. Given today's cost of photographic materials, my accuracy saved my employer about twenty-five dollars each week. And, unlike my coworkers, I required no supervision by my employer."*

Particularly for jobs in the private sector, assets should be translated into dollars, whenever possible. The areas of efficiency and productivity are particularly amenable to this kind of translation.

Speed of Learning. Employers are also interested in how quickly an employee can grasp new materials and skills. An employee who is still learning is not really "earning."

When Nancy went to work at Ampco, she was assigned to a coworker who taught her the ropes. It took Nancy just a week to reach the point where she could work independently. Later, Nancy watched some new people being trained. To her surprise, Nancy found that it took the new people two weeks to get squared away! She asked around and found that two weeks was "standard." Thus, Nancy can say that she was able to learn the job twice as quickly as company policy allowed for.

Practice Situations

Now that you have had an opportunity to see some examples of how client assets can be identified, you can practice developing your own skills in this area. As before, your initial practice can involve developing indicators of your own ability to do the job. Work with whatever job you have had that is most relevant to your own career. Organize your information in a manner similar to Table 8.

Table 8.   Practice Exercise in Developing Indicators of Ability to Do the Job

Productivity: _____

_____

_____

_____

Recognition: _____

_____

_____

_____

Efficiency and accuracy: _____

_____

_____

_____

Speed of learning: _____

_____

_____

_____

Second, practice by working with a client or a friend to identify the indicators of his/her ability to do the job, using the four subareas as stimuli. Give some appropriate examples for each subarea, and begin to explore each question with the person. Do not forget to respond to the input you receive. If the client has the capability, it is best if he/she records the assets in writing. This will help to keep the client involved and to promote a feeling that the results are hers/his.

Proving That the Client Is a Dependable Worker

In many professional positions, the employee's dependability is assumed, and the client will not need to demonstrate that fact. However, an employer's concern about dependability may be heightened if the employer is aware of the client's previous psychiatric disability. In those nonprofessional positions in which employee turnover and absenteeism are common problems, the client's ability to identify assets in this area can be a definite plus.

Again, there are four subareas within this particular asset area: (1) attendance, (2) promptness, (3) speed of production, and (4) use of time.

Attendance. How was the client's attendance at work? If the client missed only a few days — or none at all — he/she will want to communicate this to prospective employers. *(Note:* An absence rate of less than one-half day per month is considered good.)

Les is able to say: *"I missed only three days of work during the past year."* Helga, who actually missed quite a few days, is still able to say in complete honesty: *"I had fewer absences than 70 percent of my coworkers."*

Promptness. Perhaps the client's attendance record was not exceptionally good — but he/she was prompt on all those days when he/she went to work. Although not as strong as a good attendance record, this fact is usable and even valuable.

Bill, a former dry-cleaning worker, is able to say: *"I was not late for work once during the days I worked last year."* And Roger can say: *"I was on time more frequently than 80 percent of my coworkers."*

Speed of Production. Is the client consistently able to complete work assignments within required time limits? Or even better — did she/he regularly complete jobs in less than the allotted time? If so, this is the kind of information that will convince employers of the client's value.

Lew's previous job was in a factory. During each eight-hour shift he was expected to assemble no fewer than 400 units. Following his training period, Lew found that he was able to complete his 400 units in about seven hours. Only four of the other employees were able to do this. Lew then explored, *"How long did it take my coworkers to do this job?"* and decided that 90 percent of them took an hour longer than he did. *"How well did I assemble my units?"* and *"How did my units compare in quality with my coworkers' units?"* Lew had a 2 percent reject rate — the same as his coworkers who took longer. Thus, Lew can say: *"I took an hour less time to assemble 400 units than 90 percent of my coworkers — with the same degree of precision and accuracy."*

Use of Time. Employers are always concerned with how their employees make use of their time: It is possible to be on the job physically and yet be doing very little actual work. A person may sit at a desk for hours, daydreaming and accomplishing little, or a person's "work" day may be squeezed between late arrival, morning coffee break, long lunch, afternoon break, and early departure. The question is, then: How did the client make use of his/her time on the job?

Maria explores the question: *"How much of my work day did I spend actually working?"* She answers truthfully: seven and a half hours out of eight hours. Then she asks: *"How did this compare with my coworkers' use of time?"* Again, she answers truthfully: None of them actually worked more than seven hours; they all took coffee breaks while she did not. Thus, she can say: *"I consistently spent 6 percent more time actually working than my coworkers who were on the job for the same period of time."*

Paul was extremely conscientious. Whenever he had a job to finish, he would cut his lunch period short or even come to work early and stay late in order to finish. He can legitimately say: *"I never failed to complete a job, even when this meant working on my own time without extra pay."*

Practice Situations

Now you can practice your skill in developing concrete and comparative factual assets in the area of dependability. Continue to use as your example the job that is most relevant to your future, recording your assets in a format similar to Table 9. When you have completed this exercise, practice identifying the dependability assets of a client or a friend. Overview what you are going to do by explaining the three basic questions and the four subareas. As you get to each subarea, give some examples. Then, explore the areas in detail with the client. Respond to the client to indicate that you are really hearing what she/he is saying. As indicated earlier, it is best if the client can record the final results.

Proving That the Client Gets Along with Others

Many employees lose or leave their jobs because of poor interpersonal relationships with coworkers or supervisors. Therefore, it can be extremely beneficial for a client with a previous psychiatric disability to be able to identify assets in this area. Like the other two areas, this

Table 9. Practice Exercise in Identifying Dependability Assets

Attendance: _____

_____

_____

_____

Promptness: _____

_____

_____

_____

Speed of production: _____

_____

_____

_____

Use of time: _____

_____

_____

_____

final area contains four subareas: (1) commendations, (2) leadership, (3) relationship with supervisor, and (4) relationship with coworkers.

Commendations. Did the client ever receive an award, positive letter, or citation that would indicate an ability to get along with others? If so, this is an important piece of information for the client's ultimate application. In addition to such formal indicators, informal commendations should also be explored.

For example, Jim remembered that a number of his customers had complimented him on his friendly manner. He guessed that over the past year and a half he had received about twenty compliments. Therefore, he could say, *"I received at least one compliment a month from customers about my friendly and helpful manner."*

Sam worked as a waiter in an ice-cream and sandwich shop. In an effort to improve the quality of service in the shop, the manager instituted a "Waiter of the Month" award, which recognized individual workers for their cheerful, prompt, and courteous interaction with customers. During the year he worked there, Sam was named Waiter of the Month three separate times. Sam asks himself: *"How did this compare with my coworkers?"* None of his eight coworkers received the award more than twice. Thus, Sam can say: *"I was the only employee who was named Waiter of the Month three different times."*

Leadership. Did the client ever have an opportunity to serve in a leadership capacity of any sort while on the job? Again, this is important information; many employers feel that leadership is a desirable quality in applicants.

Martha was asked on several occasions to oversee the training of new employees. She explores: *"How many times was I asked to train others?"* She served in this capacity on ten different occasions. *"How did this compare with my coworkers?"* None of Martha's coworkers was asked to conduct training programs more than five times. Thus, Martha can say: *"I was asked to serve as the leader of training groups of new employees twice as often as any of my coworkers."*

Relationship with Supervisor. How did the client get along with her/his coworkers? A relationship with any coworker can be better-than-average relationship, this fact is definitely usable. A relationship with an employer or supervisor can be characterized as "better than average" if the employer never came in conflict with the client, if the employer tended to talk with the client more than with other employees about things not directly related to the job, and if the client was willing to do things for this employer that he/she would not have done for other employers.

Sharon's supervisor recognized that she and Sharon had many things in common. For example, they came from the same part of the country. The supervisor developed the habit of stopping at Sharon's desk for casual conversation. They got on well together. Sharon remembers this and says: *"I had a better-than-average relationship with my supervisor."*

Relationship with Coworkers. How did the client get along with her/his coworkers? A relationship with an coworker can be characterized as "better than average" if that coworker tended to come to the client for help and advice, if the coworker automatically included the client in his/her discussion and planning, and if the coworker frequently singled the client out for general companionship.

Ralph did not do too well in relating to his boss. As a matter of fact, they had several arguments about the best method of handling particular jobs. However, Ralph's independence and strength won him the admiration of many of his coworkers. He can honestly say: *"I enjoyed a better-than-average relationship with 85 percent of my coworkers on my last job."*

27

Practice Situations

Practice your own skill in discovering assets that prove you get along with others. Begin by using your own most relevant job experience. Record your assets in a manner similar to Table 10. Once this has been completed, practice finding the relevant assets of a client or a friend. Do not forget to overview the process by reminding him/her of the questions, telling him/her about the subareas, and then giving an example in each subarea as you come to it. Be sure to respond to the content and/or feeling the client expresses during the exploration.

Table 10. Practice Exercise in Identifying Relating Assets

Commendations: _____

_____

_____

_____ _____

Leadership activities: _____

_____

_____

_____

Relationship with supervisor: _____

_____

_____

_____

Relationship with coworkers: _____

_____

_____

_____

IDENTIFYING ASSETS FROM EDUCATIONAL EXPERIENCE

The goal of this section is precisely the same as that of the previous work-experience section: to enable the practitioner to help the clients to identify concrete facts that are indicative of their ability to perform the job, to be dependable employees, and to relate effectively to people in the work environment. Here, however, the clients will explore their educational background.

The same strategy that was used earlier will be followed here. That is, practitioner and client will ask and answer variants of the basic questions.

1. *Quantitative:* How much or how many did the client do/make/handle here?

2. *Qualitative:* How well did the client do in this area?

3. *Comparative:* How did the client's quantitative or qualitative performance compare with that of other students or trainees?

As before, the concrete facts can be stated in terms of numbers or appropriate symbols *("I maintained a B+ average"),* percentages *("I completed more assignments on time than 75 percent of my fellow students"),* absolute words *("I was never late to class"),* or amounts *("I rebuilt three different engines in my auto mechanics class").*

The identification of assets from educational experience is clearly a recycling process. It needs to be completed only if (1) the client's educational experience is more relevant to the career goal than past work experience, (2) the performance indicators from the client's work experience are weak, or (3) the educational-experience indicators are strong and could thus make the client a more attractive prospect.

The remainder of this chapter will focus on using the quantitative, qualitative, and comparative questions to find specific factual assets in the client's past educational experience. As suggested above, this section will have considerable overlap with the previous section. In order to minimize repetition, only those subareas that are unique will be addressed.

Proving That the Client Can Do the Job

This area contains four subareas to be explored with the client: (1) grades, (2) recognition, (3) performance skills, and (4) speed of learning. The subareas of recognition and speed of learning were analyzed in the work-experience section and will not be repeated here. Therefore, only grades and performance skills will be discussed.

Grades. Information about the client's grades in school can be presented in one of two ways: by citing the actual grade average, or by referring to the client's class standing. If neither of these presents the client in an attractive light, the client can simply state the number of high grades received or indicate how many students received fewer high grades. *Information about the client's grades should be presented in the most positive light.* In general, any grade average above B- is usable, as is any figure that places the client in at least the top 30 percent of the group or class. Grades and class standing can be calculated for any of the following four categories: performance in all courses; performance in job-related courses; performance in a single course; performance in one part of one course. *The first two are more important than the last two.* The last two can be used only if the client is unable to gather information from the first two.

1. **Performance in all courses:** Frank, who wants to work for the post office, asks himself the first question: *"How many grades did I earn last year?"* His answer is ten — one for each of the ten courses he took. *"How did this compare with other students?"* Other students tended to take the same number of courses and receive the same number of grades. John's answers here failed to distinguish him. So he then asks: *"How well did I perform in this area?"* He calculates his average for all courses and finds that it is an A-. *"How did my performance compare with that of other students?"* Checking with the registrar's office, John finds that his average put him in the top 8 percent of his class. The answers to these last two questions make John stand out and thus are very usable.

2. **Performance in job-related courses:** Lucille's work in job-related courses was much better than her work in other courses, so she focuses on the former. *"How many grades did I receive in job-related courses?"* She received grades in twelve job-related courses. *"How did this compare with other students?"* Most other students took no more than nine job-related courses. Lucille can now say: *"I took 33 percent more job-related courses than most other students."* *"How well did I perform in this area?"* Lucille's average in job-related courses was a B. *"How did my performance compare with other students?"* Lucille's average put her in the top 27 percent of students in her job area. Thus, Lucille can use three of her four answers to these questions — or perhaps even all four.

3. **Performance in a single course:** Ralph's overall and job-related grades were not exceptional. However, he did very well in *one* job-related course, metal shop. He sees that the answers to the first two questions will not be helpful to him. Therefore, he proceeds to another question: *"How well did I perform in this area?"* Ralph checks back with his old shop teacher and finds

that only one other student in the class of twenty received grades as high as his. Thus, Ralph can say: *"I earned an A- in metal shop and was in the top 10 percent of the class."*

4. **Performance in one part of one course:** Lynn, who wants to be a medical technician, took a biology course that was part lecture, part lab. She did not do well in the lecture part, but she did extremely well in the lab section. She asks: *"How well did I perform in this area?"* Lynn had an A- average on her lab reports. *"How did my performance compare with other students?"* Lynn's averages were the highest in the class. She can write: *"My A- average in the laboratory section of this biology course was the highest in the class."*

Performance Skills. Many employers want to know what types of operations clients can perform and how well they can perform them. In many cases, this will require clients to indicate in specific terms the machines they can run or the specific processes they can handle.

Ellen plans to indicate that she can set up and operate both single-color and two-color printing presses — and that her set-up time in class was faster than 75 percent of her fellow students. Ben, who wants a job as an apprentice carpenter, has learned to use all the basic hand and power tools in woodworking. Sara learned to type 65 words a minute, take shorthand at 105 words per minute, and operate all basic office machines including the Flexowriter and the Verifax duplicator. Harry, who can perform every basic type of auto repair, can do a minor tune-up on an eight-cylinder car in fifteen minutes less than the book time.

Proving That the Client Is a Dependable Worker

Again, there are four subareas within this larger area: (1) attendance, (2) promptness, (3) completion of work, and (4) participation. The first three subareas are similar to those in the work-experience section. Therefore, only participation will be covered here.

Participation. How much and how well did the client participate in his/her courses and extracurricular activities? If the level of participation was high, this fact may be valuable: employers usually like people who are involved.

After going back over his educational summary and reflecting on each of his classes, Joe can legitimately say: *"I was a more frequent participant in my economics class discussion than any of my fellow students."* Gwyn writes: *"I was involved every day in discussions in my community health class and was called on eight different times to act as discussion leader."* And Bob says: *"During my senior year, I was an active member of three different clubs."*

Proving That the Client Gets Along with Others

As in all the other areas, there are four subareas: (1) commendations, (2) leadership, (3) relationship with teachers, and (4) relationship with other students. Since all of these subareas are similar to the subareas in the work-experience section, they do not need elaboration here.

Once the practitioner becomes knowledgeable about the client's assets, he/she can vary the level of client involvement in the career placement process. Clients whose work and educational summary indicates a potentially high number of assets can be presented in the overview of the task as in Table 11. After the practitioner provides some examples of the process, those clients might be able to develop a number of assets on their own. In contrast, clients who have problematic work and educational summaries need not be presented with all twenty-four subareas. Their inability to identify assets in a number of the subareas may hamper their feelings of competence and confidence — the opposite of what asset identification seeks to accomplish. For these clients,

Table 11. Asset Areas from Work and Educational Experience

Work	*Education*
I. Can the client do the job?	
1. Productivity	1. Grades
2. Recognition	2. Recognition
3. Efficiency and accuracy	3. Performance skills
4. Speed of learning	4. Speed of learning
II. Is the client dependable?	
1. Attendance	1. Attendance
2. Promptness	2. Promptness
3. Speed of production	3. Completion of work
4. Use of time	4. Participation
III. Can the client get along with others?	
1. Commendations	1. Commendations
2. Leadership	2. Leadership
3. Relationship with supervisor	3. Relationship with teachers
4. Relationship with coworkers	4. Relationship with students

the practitioner may present the subareas to the client one at a time, beginning with the area in which the practitioner suspects that the client has some assets. In this manner, almost all clients, no matter how inadequate their job or educational history, can identify several assets. Experience in sheltered workshop settings, transitional employment, and the like are quite helpful in providing the client with a work or training experience from which they can identify assets (Bean and Beard, 1975),

Practice Situations

As the final practice exercise in developing your own asset identification skills, review your own most relevant educational experience for indicators of your ability to do the desired job, function dependably, and get along with other people. Record this information in a format similar to Table 12. Then round out your practice by working with a client or a friend to dig out assets from a relevant educational experience. Overview the process by defining concrete facts; going over the quantitative, qualitative, and comparative questions; and explaining the three major asset areas. As you get to each subarea, give relevant examples. Finally, explore the subarea with the person and respond to the content and/or feeling that the exploration elicits. Remember that the client will be more actively involved if she/he makes the actual written record of the assets developed.

IDENTIFYING CLIENT ASSETS FROM WORK AND EDUCATIONAL EXPERIENCE: A SUMMARY

Goal: To identify concrete facts in the client's job experience and educational background that indicate his/her ability to perform the job, to be a dependable employee, and to relate effectively to others in the work environment.

1. Overview the process with the client by explaining the qualitative, quantitative, and comparative questions; the three major asset areas; and the respective subareas.

2. Give relevant examples for each subarea and explore the subarea with the client.

3. Respond to the information presented by the client by responding to the client's feeling, content, or both.

4. Identify the assets and state them in concrete and factual terms.

5. If possible, have the client record the assets.

**Table 12. Practice Exercise in Identifying Assets from a
Relevant Educational Experience**

Can the client do the job?

Grades: _____

_____

Recognition: _____

_____

Performance skills: _____

_____

Speed of learning: _____

_____

Is the client dependable?

Attendance: _____

_____

Promptness: _____

_____

Completion of work: _____

_____

Participation: _____

_____

Can the client get along with others?

Commendations: _____

_____

Leadership: _____

_____

Relationship with teachers: _____

_____

Relationship with students: _____

_____

_____

_____

EXPLORING ASSETS: A SKILLED APPROACH

There wasn't anything special about Brad — or so he felt, at least. Since his release from the hospital, he had been receiving counseling from Clara on an outpatient basis. She had been quite pleased with the way he had regained a real degree of self-confidence. Faced with the prospect of looking for work, however, Brad now seemed in danger of losing everything he had gained.

"Ah, they're not even going to talk to a jerk like me," he told Clara, gesturing to the advertisement she had clipped from that morning's paper.

"I know you feel really helpless because you don't have any experience in just this area," Clara responded. "But after all, 'vending machine salesman' was right at the top of that list of possible jobs that we drew up together. And this ad says that Samson, Incorporated, is looking for exactly that kind of salesman."

"Yeah, I know," Brad said glumly. "But let's face it — I never sold supplies for vending machines in my life. There's bound to be a whole lot of guys applying who are real pros. I wouldn't have a chance!"

But Clara felt sure that Brad would have a chance. And she was determined to see that he made the most of that chance. After talking with him for a few minutes, she introduced the idea of exploring his occupational assets.

"What do you mean, my assets?" The idea confused Brad at first, but Clara was able to clear up this confusion quickly.

"Sure, previous experience is one important thing that most employers look for right away," she said. "But it's not the only thing. In many cases, an employer is even more concerned with what kind of worker you are in general. What we need to do is explore some ways of showing your strengths — and doing it in such a way that Samson ends up being willing to overlook your lack of specific experience."

"Yeah?" Brad may have been unconvinced, but he was clearly interested. "It sounds good. How do we do it?"

*"We give them **proof** of how well you've done in the past," Clara said. "We take a good, long look at your past jobs, your outside activities — everything we can. And we come up with as many hard-and-fast facts as we can to show that you're the best person for this particular job."*

And this is precisely what they did, beginning with Brad's earlier jobs. He had already mentioned that he had worked as a door-to-door salesman sometime before. With Clara's help, he remembered that his own sales during the first four months of the job had been nearly double those of the salesmen who had started work at the same time.

"I never thought about that before," he said. "Hey, that makes me sound pretty good, huh?" As they moved on, there was real enthusiasm in his new exploration.

"Listen, I've got something," he exclaimed after a few more minutes. "For a job like this you've got to do a lot of driving, right? Well, you're looking at a guy with an A-number-one, perfect driving record! Not one accident in fourteen years of driving — not even a ticket!"

"That's beautiful," Clara said, grinning and taking notes furiously. "And listen, didn't you say you never used to get sick on the jobs you had like a lot of the other men?"

"Right, right!" Brad nodded vigorously. "Sure — that's how I did so good on my door-to-door job! I only missed one day the whole time I worked there. Those other guys, they must have been out three or four times a month!"

"Missed only one day on job," Clara murmured as she wrote, "lowest absentee rate of all employees ... "

In the end it was a cheerful, confident Brad who walked out of Clara's office that day. After several more sessions with Clara, he headed for Samson, Incorporated. And if Clara's strong streak of practical realism kept her from feeling totally confident, she still felt far more pleasure than surprise when Brad called the next day, his voice high and excited. "Hey, guess what!" he exclaimed. "I got the job! I did!" And Clara, hanging up at last, thought, "Sure you did. There's something special about all of us if we just know how to look for it."

Chapter 3 *UNDERSTANDING THE CLIENT'S WORK OPPORTUNITIES*

UNDERSTANDING OPPORTUNITIES: AN UNSKILLED APPROACH

"OK, Robert," Barbara said, moving back behind her desk and sitting down. "You know you're getting near the end of this treatment process. Things are really looking up for you. The only major thing that's left is to help you to get a job — something that you'll enjoy and something that'll let you feel you're really earning your own keep instead of depending on other people."

"Sure . . ." Robert, a young man with dark, watchful eyes and an expression of unfailing defensiveness, nodded his agreement. "I want to go to work. But what — ?"

"Well now, you've talked a lot about your interest in auto mechanics," Barbara reminded him, her voice businesslike and confident. "From what you've said, you probably have the ability to be a regular mechanic."

Robert shrugged. "Yeah, probably, I guess. Only — well, without any real experience, I doubt anyone would want to hire me. Would they?"

"Perhaps not as a mechanic — at least not right away. You'd probably have to start off as a gas station attendant and work your way up. How would you feel about that?"

Robert considered that for a moment, then nodded. "Yeah. Yeah, that'd be OK. I wouldn't mind that."

"Fine!" Barbara scratched some notes on her pad. "Well, then, the first thing you ought to do is start checking the 'Help Wanted' ads for possible openings."

"Uh-huh. But — what if there aren't any?"

"Well, then you can check with the state employment office. You know where that is — over on Federal?" Robert nodded. "And you might also talk to some of the gas station managers near where you live. With those three approaches, you certainly should be able to find something."

But, as Robert discovered, there was a considerable gap between "should" and "could." Although the local newspaper's "Help Wanted" column advertised two appropriate openings during the next week, both were for jobs at gas stations well outside the city limits — and thus outside Robert's range of possible commutation. Lacking his own car, he had to depend on bus service to get places. And the buses, alas, went nowhere near either of these two stations.

Robert did check out job openings advertised through the State Em-

ployment Service. Unfortunately, the few openings listed there involved qualifications he simply did not have — such as a minimum of one year of previous experience. Hoping against hope that something would materialize, he talked with two or three station managers near his home. But none of these places was hiring. Tired and discouraged, he could only stare at Barbara with dark disappointment during their next session as she valiantly tried to boost his spirits.

"It's not the end of the world," she kept telling him. But, deep inside, Robert's private voice kept answering, "Maybe not your world — but you ought to try living in mine!"

Once clients know *what* they have to offer a potential employer, they need specific understanding of *where* these assets can be offered. The major client deficit addressed in this chapter, therefore, is the lack of specific information about where the desired position may be obtained.

Competition for jobs is an overwhelming reality in today's employment situation: very few good jobs have only one applicant. Part of the process of preparing psychiatrically disabled clients to compete for a job is helping them to understand the assets they have to offer. This is the "qualitative" dimension in preparation. However, there is also a "quantitative" dimension in effective competition. The more places in which the client seeks a desired position, the better the chances are that the position will be obtained. Thus, the practitioner will want to help clients who are deficient in this area to identify as many potential places of employment as possible.

Furthermore, some psychiatrically disabled clients need to discard their narrow concepts of the alternatives available to them. They need to expand the world of possibilities and overcome the defeatist stance that is often reflected in such questions as "Who would want to hire me, anyway?" For these clients, the understanding process of career placement can develop new and positive insights into the world of reality.

The three major steps involved in the employer-identification process are: (1) *determining geographical limits,* (2) *identifying the sources of advertised job openings,* and (3) *identifying the unadvertised jobs.*

DETERMINING GEOGRAPHICAL LIMITS

The geographical area where the client is willing and/or able to work is a key factor in delimiting potential employment possibilities. Therefore, the practitioner will want to help the client to determine where she/he will be residing and any attendant travel limitations. In particular, the practitioner will need to clarify (1) where the client will live, (2) whether the client will be willing to move to an area where there may be greater job possibilities, (3) whether the client will have her/his own transportation or will be relying on public transportation, and (4) what the commuting limitations are in terms of time or distance.

For example, Arnie doesn't want to move. He presently has no car of his own but wishes to find work as a heavy-equipment operator. Consequently, he defines his geographical target area like this: *"An in-town company that I can get to each morning by either bus or subway in one hour."* By calling the transportation companies, he can find out if there are any areas of the city he must eliminate.

Margo, who wants to find work as a computer programmer, has her own means of transportation. She defines her desired geographical area as follows: *"A company within one hour's drive of my apartment."* By looking at a map, she is able to find what towns lie within her geographical range.

In helping the client to set geographical limits, it is important to be realistic about the employment possibilities within that area. For example, Margo lives in a residential area and would love to work for a company only minutes away. In order to increase her chances, however, she sets her geographical limits so as to take in the greatest number of possible employers. Margo's feeling is that "It's better to *have* a job far away than to have *no* job close to home!" Bob would agree. He wants a job as an inhalation therapist. He has decided that his best chance for a job will be in a city that is fairly large — over 50,000 people. He consults a map to identify such cities in his state. He will continue to use the map to identify and locate smaller towns if he feels this will improve his chances of finding work.

Practice Situations

Using the above "think steps" as a guideline, identify the geographical location within which you would be willing to seek future employment. Then, work with a friend or a client to identify the geographical location within which he/she would be willing to engage in a job search.

IDENTIFYING ADVERTISED JOB OPENINGS

At this point, the practitioner has helped the client to understand what she/he has to offer and to develop a general idea of where to look for employment. The next step is to begin identifying specific employers who might employ the client in a preferred position.

Advertised job openings refer to those jobs that are being advertised publicly in newspapers, employment agencies, or other sources. These openings should be checked out first. If the client can obtain a desired job through one of these sources, the time and energy invested by both the practitioner and the client will be minimized.

Each of the following represents a common source of advertised job listings:

1. Newspapers
2. Trade/professional publications and newsletters (available at most libraries)
3. State employment office
4. Private employment agencies (general or specialized)
5. Relevant labor and professional organizations
6. School counseling and/or placement offices (many are open to all alumni)
7. City Hall (CETA and other manpower programs administered through the city)
8. Local office of the U.S. Deparment of Labor (apprenticeship and veterans' programs administered by this agency)

To help the client effectively, the practitioner will want to examine the above categories and identify the specific sources that are relevant to the client's career goal. For an agency, this would mean answering the following questions.

1. *What* is the specific source? (E.g., Massachusetts State Employment Service Job Center)
2. *Where* is it located? (E.g., 253 Huntington Avenue)
3. *Who* is the contact person? (Preferably name and position, but at least position — e.g., Mr. Joe Callahan, Veterans' Counselor)
4. *How* can he be contacted? (E.g., phone 727-6320)
5. *How* do you use the source? (Application, interview, review of relevant job openings, screening, referral, employer contact)

For a written source such as a newspaper, the only questions that usually need be answered are "What is the specific source?" and "How do you use the source?"

The "How do you use the source" question will help the practitioner to ensure that the client is really prepared to use the source. For example, in order to use the employment service effectively, the client needs to know exactly what she/he is looking for. If the employment interviewer screens clients, the client will need to be prepared to present his/her assets. The practitioner can prepare the client to use the source by explaining what to do, demonstrating how to do it, and then having the client practice doing it. Book 6 of this series describes in specific detail the process involved in effectively linking a client to a community resource.

Practice Situations

As a practice exercise, list the specific sources you could use to identify advertised job openings of interest to you. Then, for at least one individual or agency source and one written source, answer the appropriate questions. Record this information about sources in a format similar to Table 13. When you have completed this exercise for yourself, work with a client or a friend to identify sources of advertised job openings for him/her.

Table 13.   Practice Exercise in Answering Basic Source
            Questions

Agency Source

> What source?
>
> Where located?
>
> Whom to contact?
>
> How to contact?
>
> How to use?

Written Source

> What source?
>
> How to use?

IDENTIFYING UNADVERTISED JOB OPENINGS

At this point, practitioner and client will want to decide what course of action to take in trying to secure a position. One alternative is to start by using the sources of advertised job openings. Of course, if the client is deficient in job application skills, the practitioner will need to prepare the client for this application process before actually initiating the job search (see Chapter 4 herein). A second alternative is to delay using sources until a comprehensive list of all the potential positions has been developed (both advertised and unadvertised). A third alternative is to begin using the advertised sources of job openings immediately — assuming the client is prepared for the application process — while simultaneously working to identify the sources of unadvertised jobs.

Each of these alternatives has specific advantages and disadvantages. The major advantage of the first alternative (beginning immediately to use the sources of advertised job openings) is that it is the most efficient in terms of time and effort. If a good job is advertised, this is the fastest way to get to it. The major disadvantage is that only a limited number of employers are contacted by the client. This may mean that the client will remain unaware of the best available job. The major advantage of the second alternative (waiting until all potential employers have been identified) is that it permits the client to become aware of all the employment possibilities. This process will generate the most possibilities and will give the client the most alternatives to choose among. In short, chances for employment are maximized. The major disadvantage is that the process of generating unadvertised job sources and contacting them is time-consuming and may mean more work for the client and the practitioner. Also, there may be a two- or three-week delay before the actual application process can be initiated. The major advantage of the third alternative (beginning immediately but also looking for unadvertised jobs) is that all possibilities are explored and the time delay is reduced. The disadvantage is that, if the client gets an offer early in the application process, he/she may not have all the information needed to make a decision and may accept a moderately acceptable job only to have a better position materialize a few weeks later.

The main consideration in deciding whether or not to search for unadvertised jobs may be summarized as follows: if the advertised job openings are few in number, or if competition is very stiff, the practitioner will want to help clients to expand their alternatives.

At this point, then, the clients will be aware of their job objectives, the assets they have to offer prospective employers, the geographical area in which they want to work, and some sources of listed job openings. The task of identifying unadvertised job openings involves expanding the potential sources of employment. More specifically, clients will need a list of twenty-five to a hundred employers — depending upon the exact nature of the job — to really maximize employment opportunity.

If the client is looking for work as a gas station attendant, for example, the final list may include as many as a hundred prospective employers; although there are many gas stations, it is unlikely that any employ more than a few people. If the client is looking for a job as a typist, on the other hand, the final list may include no more than twenty-five large companies, each of which employs dozens of typists. In other words, the client will need to develop his/her job list according to how many potential jobs the total number of prospective employers represents. As a general rule, the greater the number of possible jobs the list represents, the greater the client's chances of obtaining one of those jobs.

The primary purpose of the job list is to establish where to send the applications. The list has several important secondary purposes, however. It can be used to gather information about potential employers, in order to estimate the client's employment chances with a particular company. The job list may also provide information that will be helpful to the client during the interview itself. The remainder of this section will focus on the steps involved in developing a comprehensive list of unadvertised job openings.

IDENTIFYING GENERAL TYPES OF COMPANIES AND ORGANIZATIONS

First, the practitioner and the client will want to explore the question: "What *types* of companies or organizations are likely to employ people in the client's job area?" Any information about such companies is essential. Good sources for such information are the *Occupational Outlook Handbook,* professional employment counselors (e.g., State Employment Service counselors), and workers in the field. In the end, the client will want to identify five to ten *types* of companies or organizations that might employ the client. As the process of exploring various sources of information about specific employers begins, these types of companies will serve as reference headings. Below are examples of types of companies/organizations that two clients worked out with their practitioner.

Arnie found that the following types of organizations would be likely to employ heavy-equipment operators:

1. Cement contractors
2. General contractors
3. Building contractors
4. Contractors' equipment companies
5. Department of Public Works
6. Highway departments

Margo discovered that these types of businesses would have use for a computer programmer:

1. Insurance companies
2. Retail mail-order companies
3. Banks
4. Social service agencies
5. Accounting firms
6. Computer companies
7. Large department stores
8. Colleges
9. Airlines
10. Government agencies

Practice Situations

As your first practice exercise, develop a list of five to ten types of organizations or companies where you might apply for the kind of job you want (see Table 14). Then, work with a client or a friend to identify types of places where she/he might find employment. Remember to overview what you are doing and to respond to the input you receive.

Table 14.   Practice Exercise in Identifying Types of Companies and Organizations for Employment

Types of Companies and Organizations

1. _____
2. _____
3. _____
4. _____
5. _____
6. _____
7. _____
8. _____
9. _____
10. _____

LISTING SPECIFIC COMPANIES AND ORGANIZATIONS

Having identified the *general* types of companies or organizations that might employ the client, the practitioner and the client will want to collect information about the *particular* companies or organizations that the client will contact.

Each entry in the final job list should include the following information:

1. Company name and address (including ZIP code)
2. Name and title of the top person (e.g., owner, president, director)
3. Telephone number

4. Total number of employees

5. Products made, services offered, and so on

Table 15 illustrates a sample format for recording this information.

Table 15. Information about Potential Employer

Name/title of top person:	Mr. Peprini, President
Name of company:	Peprini Corporation
Street address of company:	73 Mt. Wayte Avenue
City, state, and ZIP code:	Framingham, Massachusetts 01701
Phone number:	(617) 875-6171
Number of employees:	Over 500
Company products or services:	Excavation, road building, steel construction, building demolition

In order to develop a comprehensive list of potential employers, the practitioner and the client may have to use several sources. Each of these is discussed below.

Yellow Pages

The Yellow Pages of the telephone book may represent the single best source for identifying potential employers. They offer a convenient, detailed list of companies organized according to the type of service or product provided. The Yellow Pages are especially useful when the client's prospective geographic location is limited to an area covered by half a dozen telephone books or less. This is usually the case. If out-of-town phone books are needed, the local library usually has them; or they can be obtained through the business office of the telephone company.

Usually, the Yellow Pages give the name of the company, the complete address (ZIP codes usually precede the Yellow Pages), and the telephone number. Yellow Pages usually do *not* supply the number of employees, the name of the top person, or the products and services — although the advertisement for an organization may give this information. The name of the top person is needed because this is the person to whom the client will ultimately send an application. This procedure results in the application being delivered to the personnel department "from the top." Below is the list of titles for top people in different organizations.

1. Factory: Plant manager or plant superintendent

2. Large business or corporation: President

3. Small business: Owner
4. Hospital or nursing home: Administrator
5. Community agency: Director
6. Hotel or motel: Manager
7. School system: Superintendent

It will be recalled that the clients will want to know the number of employees in order to understand the likelihood of employment. Knowledge of the services and products allows the clients to determine whether or not a particular business employs any people in the type of work they desire. One way to fill in these informational gaps is to simply make a phone call to the organization and ask for the necessary information.

To the extent possible, clients should be responsible for developing their own lists of potential employers. The client's level of functioning will, of course, be the determining factor, but most clients will be able to use the Yellow Pages effectively on their own, once they have been taught the fundamentals. Thus, the practitioner can make the best use of his/her time by initially assisting clients and then allowing them to do the rest of the work as a "homework" assignment. Specifically, then, the practitioner will want to make sure that the client knows the phonebook heading under which each of his/her types of companies is found. Then the practitioner can show the client how to record the information. The client can then practice recording information on the job list. Finally, the practitioner can teach the client how to make phone calls to employers to obtain needed information. Again, this requires explaining what to ask for, demonstrating how to do it, and having the client rehearse with the practitioner and then practice with an employer or two. After this "learning" period, the client will be able to carry out the rest of the assignment independently.

Manufacturers' Directories

A manufacturers' directory is published for most states (e.g., the *New York Manufacturers' Directory,* the *Illinois Manufacturers' Directory).* These directories often have slightly different titles, and some cover more than one state. (Persons located in one of the New England states, for example, can use the *Directory of New England Manufacturers.*) Originally intended for use by salespeople, the directories provide a wealth of information about *industrial companies* in each state: company name, address, telephone number; name and title of top person; number of employees; type of goods produced — in other words, everything that is needed to make complete entries on the job list. Thus, these directories can be used to complete information gathered from the Yellow Pages about *industrial* employers. If the client is interested in jobs in an industrial setting, the directory can also be used to expand the employer possibilities. The directory is particularly useful if the client is willing to explore a large area for possible job opportunities (say, a whole state). The directory is also very useful if the client wishes to work at a job that can be found in many industries. For example, a carpenter might find employment as a maintenance worker in any large industry. A factory assembler could also be employed in a wide range of industrial settings. Finally, the directory can be used to make sure that all potential employers of a given type have been accounted for in the Yellow Pages search.

All manufacturers' directories list individual companies in three ways: *(a)* alphabetically by name; *(b)* geographically; *(c)* according to specific products. The alphabetical and geographical sections of the manufacturers' directory are not difficult to use. After checking a map for the specific towns that are in the client's chosen geographical area, one can simply turn to the desired section in the directory and read about the companies that are listed.

The section that lists companies according to their specific products — and this is the section where the *types* of companies will be most helpful — does require some explanation. The beginning of this section in the manufacturers' directory includes a basic list of the *types* of products manufactured by different companies. Each type of product is coded. The list at the beginning of the "product" section can be consulted to find the code number or numbers for the types of companies that might employ people in the desired job area. The page indicated may then be checked to find individual companies with the appropriate code numbers. For each company, the following questions should be asked:

1. Is this company within the client's geographical area?
2. Would a company like this that produces [*type of product*] be likely to employ people in the client's job area? *(Note:* Large companies with more than a hundred employees will have people working in almost every job area. The smaller the company, the more carefully it will have to be checked to make sure that the desired work — or closely related work — is actually done at a given company.)
3. Is this company large enough that the client can reasonably expect there to be some turnover in his/her job area? *(Note:* Companies with a hundred or more employees can be rated "excellent," those with fifty to a hundred "good," those with twenty-five to fifty "fair," and those with fewer than twenty-five "poor.")

If the answer to the first two questions is yes, the client will want to enter this company on her/his list. If the company has fewer than twenty-five employees, however, it is not a very strong prospect.

As with the Yellow Pages, the manufacturers' directory can be used independently by most clients *if* the practitioner explains how to use it, demonstrates its use, and then has the client practice using it a few times under supervision.

Service Directories and Other Materials

If the client's job area is related to "service industries," a service directory may be of use. Service directories are currently published for some states (e.g., the *Illinois Service Directory*), and it seems likely that directories will be published for more states in the near future. These directories cover businesses that provide a wide range of *services* to both individuals and organizations. Service industries include hotels, restaurants, transportation services, skilled trades (e.g., carpenters, plumbers), and many types of sales services.

Service directories are arranged exactly like the manufacturers' directories but are coded by service rather than product. The procedures for using the service directory are precisely the same as those spelled out above for the manufacturers' directories.

In addition to these general directories, many areas have specialized directories. For example, the *Hotel and Motel Red Book* lists every major hotel and motel in the country. A good resource for identifying these specialized directories is the *Guide to American Directories*. The type of company to be researched can be found in the table of contents and one may then turn to the pages listed for reference to specific directories in that area.

The many *social service* organizations (schools, hospitals, public agencies, charities) comprise a final category of employers. Although most states do not publish directories that list individual social service organizations, an excellent list can be developed by checking with other sources. In many areas, for example, the United Fund (a non-profit funding agency) publishes a directory of local social service agencies. These United Fund directories provide all the information needed to compile an excellent list of social service employers in a local area. In addition, specialized groups can be contacted (the Hospital Association, for example, if the client is looking for a job in health care).

Like the manufacturers' directories, all the above resources can be used to complete information obtained from the Yellow Pages or to develop new possibilities.

One final note: if the client is having trouble developing enough entries for his/her list, there are two possibilities open.

1. The client can consider extending the geographical area within which he/she is willing to work.
2. The client can broaden the "scope" of the type of job he/she wants. (For example, Arnie might broaden "heavy-equipment operator" to include such industrial positions as forklift operator.)

Remember, one major key to getting job interviews is to contact a large number of potential employers.

Practice Situations

Now that you have learned about the sources for identifying potential employers, you can practice developing a list of potential employers for unadvertised job openings within your preferred occupational area. Try to come up with at least twenty-five. Record your information using the format of Table 15.

The information may be recorded on a file card, using one card for each unadvertised job opening. A practitioner or group of practitioners can then develop a pool of relevant information about potential sources of employment for specific job objectives.

When you have completed this exercise, work with a client or a friend to help him/her to identify potential sources of jobs. Try to pick someone to whom you can teach the use of the various sources so that you can get practice in this phase of delivery. Follow the explain-demonstrate-practice procedure spelled out earlier. It is suggested that even if the practice exercises do not require the use of material other than the Yellow Pages you should try to locate the various directories mentioned in this section and familiarize yourself with them.

UNDERSTANDING THE CLIENT'S WORK OPPORTUNITIES: A SUMMARY

Goal: To provide the client with specific information about where the desired job may be obtained.

1. Help the client to set geographical limits regarding his/her employment possibilities. Determine where the client will live and any attendant travel limitations.

2. Help the client to use the sources of advertised job openings in order to identify potential employers.

3. Help the client to identify unadvertised job openings. *(a)* Identify the general types of companies and organizations that might employ the client. *(b)* List the specific companies and organizations that might employ the client.

4. Assist the client in collecting information about potential employers (e.g., number of employees, services, products). Explain, demonstrate, and have the client practice using various sources of information.

5. Have the client develop a comprehensive list of potential employers.

UNDERSTANDING OPPORTUNITIES: A SKILLED APPROACH

If Robert nourished dreams of becoming an auto mechanic, Julia was equally attracted by the idea of becoming a chef.

"Not a cook," she kept telling Theo. "See, a chef is a whole different thing. Like, most chefs are men — don't ask me why. But they're like super-good cooks who can do all kinds of fancy things with food. And they can really make good money in the right place!"

Theo grinned. "And you feel you've got what it takes to become a chef?"

Julia shrugged. "Sure, why not? I mean, I've always been into cooking. I really know my way around. And it's the kind of work I'd really like to do."

"Great!" Theo's enthusiasm was both clear and genuine. "But without any experience — you know, a job in the past where you worked in a restaurant or something — you'll probably have to start out at the bottom."

Julia nodded. "Yeah, I guess so. I was thinking that I'd probably need a year just working anywhere as a cook before I could talk my way into even an apprentice thing in a really good restaurant. Only — only — " she looked at Theo quizzically. "How do I go about getting that first job?"

Theo grinned again. "I may not know much about fine cooking. But getting jobs is something I can help you with."

They began their campaign by deciding on the area within which Julia wanted to work. This came down to any place within twenty miles of her home that could be reached via public transportation. Then they worked together to outline the ways in which Julia could develop a list of possible employers.

"Newspaper ads are one source, of course," Theo said. "So's the state employment office. But these will only tell you about the places that are actively looking for cooks. You'll be better off if you can contact far more places. Even if they aren't advertising, they may still have a spot that could be filled. You might check out headings in the Yellow Pages section of the phone book.

"For restaurants, you mean?"

"Sure, restaurants would be natural places to list. But there are also other kinds of places that hire cooks — like large department stores that have their own employee cafeterias and customer coffee shops, or even large factories or schools. In other words, any type of place that's likely to be feeding people on a daily basis."

"Hey, that's great," Julia said. "I never would have thought of trying places like that!"

Theo's suggestion turned out to be a good one. For in the end Julia was able to list some seventy-five places within her work area that employed cooks — and this list didn't include places that Julia had learned paid poor wages! Most of the seventy-five turned out to have all the cooks they needed. But several places were definitely interested. In the end, Julia was offered a job in the small kitchen that served the Peacock Terrace, the intimate luncheon spot serving customers shopping on the fourth floor of the expensive Marcus-Newbold department store.

"I'm not a chef yet, just an assistant cook," Julia told Theo. But Theo knew that Julia's next step was only a matter of time.

Chapter 4   ACTING TO GET A JOB

ACTING TO PRESENT SELF: AN UNSKILLED APPROACH

Brady's interview was set for 2:30 at the main Cranston yard out on West Fillmore. Brady was so primed, however, that he found himself on the spot almost an hour early. He thought about going in but decided against it. Selwick, the guy he was supposed to be interviewed by, would almost certainly be busy. Early was one thing; too early was another. Spotting a coffee shop down the street, Brady walked to it and parked himself at the counter where he could keep an eye on the large wall clock.

The coffee did nothing to quiet his nervousness. Brady knew he could handle any heavy equipment that Cranston Construction might have. Heck, he had driven everything from a loader dozer to a dragline in his time. No, it wasn't the work itself that scared him. What if this guy Selwick asked what Brady had been doing recently — and learned that he had spent the last few months in a VA hospital? How would he react — and what would his reaction mean in terms of Brady's job chances?

Judith, the counselor who had been working with Brady since his release from the hospital, hadn't given him much to go on. As a matter of fact, the only thing they had really decided together was that Brady shouldn't lie about his hospital stay if the subject should come up. Maybe it wouldn't. Maybe Selwick would just ask about his experience and let it go at that. Maybe the interview would be a snap. Maybe — .

By 2:10 Brady couldn't sit still another minute. Time to go. He paid for his coffee and headed down the street toward the Cranston yard.

Selwick was ready for him, sitting at a battered desk in the company's small office and shuffling through a pile of papers.

"Brady?" His voice, though a bit gravelly, sounded friendly enough.

"Yessir, that's me." Brady hunched himself into a rickety chair and tried to look calm and collected. He watched as Selwick rummaged through the papers and came up with the application form that Brady had filled out the week before. Selwick gazed at the form thoughtfully, one hand coming to pull gently on the lobe of his ear.

"You've worked heavy stuff before, huh Brady?" he said at last, his eyes still on the form. Brady nodded vigorously.

"Yessir — I sure have!"

Selwick nodded. "Only not for quite a while, it looks like." Now he raised his eyes and looked at Brady for the first time. "It seems like you've been out of work for a while, Brady. How come? What've you been doing?"

It seemed as though a dozen answers crowded Brady's head. But even as he sorted through these, he heard a remote voice — his own — answer, "I — I've been up at the hospital."

"Yeah?" Selwick's voice wasn't unkind, only insistent. "What for?"

"D-drinking, I guess. I — I had kind of a problem."

And that was it. Although Selwick asked a few more questions about other things, Brady could sense that the real interview had ended. He couldn't think of any way to counter the damning fact of his hospitalization. All he could think was, "How come Judith didn't help me figure out how to deal with this kind of thing? How come? She's supposed to be the counselor! Didn't she know? How come she couldn't help? How come? How come?"

In general terms, the deficit addressed by this chapter is client inability to apply for a job. More specifically, this chapter deals with clients' problems in presenting themselves in writing to a potential employer in order to obtain an interview (i.e., writing a letter of introduction and résumé, filling out application forms) and presenting themselves in person to a potential employer (i.e., interviewing).

Many psychiatrically disabled clients are fearful of the job-interviewing process. They voice real concerns about their ability to present themselves in writing or in person. Whether their fears are real or not, they clearly indicate a desire to feel more confident about their self-presentations. In striking contrast to the demands of the therapeutic interviewing process, the job-interviewing process requires that clients present themselves confidently and skillfully. To accomplish this presentation, many clients need specific preparation and practice. Much of the information necessary to prepare the client to apply for a job was developed during the asset identification stage. Now, practitioner and client use this information to help write a cover letter and a résumé and prepare for the job interview.

As noted, there are two modes of client presentation required for career placement: written and personal. Each of these will be discussed.

PRESENTATION OF SELF IN WRITING

Clients who are faced with the necessity of presenting themselves effectively in writing must learn to handle four separate but related tasks: (1) developing a résumé, (2) developing a cover letter, (3) contacting employers, and (4) completing application forms. Each of these four tasks will be dealt with in turn.

DEVELOPING A RÉSUMÉ

This section focuses on what a practitioner can do to help clients to organize their work and educational assets (identified in Chapter 2) into an effective résumé. The goal of writing a résumé is to interest employers in conducting a personal interview with the client. Thus, the résumé is essentially a sales tool; it summarizes the client's experience and training in such a way as to sell his/her services to employers. As will be seen, the purposes of the résumé are several: (1) to be mailed to potential employers to solicit an interview; (2) to accompany a standard application form; (3) to facilitate the client's performance in the job interview.

The first two purposes are the more traditional. However, as suggested by the third purpose, the résumé can also be used to improve the job-interviewing skills of psychiatrically disabled clients. For clients who need to be assured that they do indeed have assets to present to an employer, the written résumé provides an observable indicator of that fact. For inarticulate clients who are unable to verbally present their assets, the written résumé can state these assets forcefully and articulately. For clients whose verbal explanations tend to be somewhat confusing or disjointed, the written résumé provides structure to "keep them on track." For these general reasons, and no doubt for other reasons relevant to individual clients, it is often important for psychiatrically disabled clients to develop a résumé — *even for those relatively unskilled jobs that typically do not require a résumé.* For many psychiatrically disabled clients, the development of a résumé has benefits over and above its more traditional rationale.

There are three important principles which the practitioner must keep in mind as the client works to draft his or her résumé:

1. *The most relevant and strongest qualifications should be presented first.* The client's first few statements or sentences are designed to grab the employer. The most convincing evidence should be right on top, not buried within the résumé.

2. *The client's important achievements and skills should be presented in an honest and direct manner.* The client should let the employer know exactly what she/he can do, without exaggerating or underrating her/his abilities.

3. *Strengths should be included and weaknesses excluded.* Like everyone else, the client has areas of weakness as well as areas of strength. The résumé, however, is not the place to mention specific weaknesses or problems. If appropriate, the client can present and explain these during a personal interview. In order to lead to an interview, however, the résumé should be a picture of strength.

In addition to adhering to these three principles, the practitioner will want to take the client through eight specific steps. These are as follows:

Step 1: Identifying self

Step 2: Identifying job goal

Step 3: Highlighting experience

Step 4: Summarizing duties and responsibilities in the most important job related experience

Step 5: Summarizing assets in the most important job-related experience

Step 6: Summarizing experience and assets in closely related areas

Step 7: Summarizing experience and assets in other relevant areas

Step 8: Supplying personal information

Two sample résumés are shown in Tables 16 and 17. Both of these clients have experienced psychiatric disabilities, with resultant gaps in their employment history. Yet each has been able to develop a résumé that contains no reference to the previous hospitalization. Although the potential employer may eventually request the more traditional, chronological type of work history, the client can be prepared to deal in person with any problems that such a request may create. In Table 16, each of the steps has been labeled. In Table 17, the steps have been developed but not labeled, so that the résumé appears in the form in which it would be used.

The résumés presented in these tables are very different from the traditional résumé format. Traditional résumés are usually constructed chronologically, starting with the most recent job and working backward. Examples of such résumés can be found in numerous U.S. Department of Labor publications. Some employers may require this type of résumé. The rehabilitation practitioner can assist the client in developing this traditional type of résumé, using as aids these various government pamphlets.

However, for reasons alluded to earlier in this chapter, many psychiatrically disabled clients can benefit from the nontraditional format of this "asset résumé." In addition, because many psychiatrically disabled clients possess a poor employment or educational history, an asset résumé may be more advantageous. In these situations, chronological résumés sometimes highlight the client's deficits rather than the client's strengths. In contrast, extended periods of unemployment and deficiencies in work experience are not readily apparent in an asset résumé. Also, those individuals who are changing to an entirely different line of work (e.g., from taxi driver to salesperson) can develop a more relevant résumé using the asset format. Housewives who have been out of the competitive work force for some time can use the asset résumé format to identify tasks inherent in their role as housewives that contain assets relevant to a wide variety of outside-of-the-home jobs.

56

Table 16. Résumé Based Primarily on Work Experience (With Steps Identified)

(Step 1) ....Mary Jones
          56 Hilltop Drive
          Anytown, CO 80990
          (909) 323-4721

JOB GOAL

(Step 2) ....Clerical Position

SUMMARY OF JOB EXPERIENCE

(Step 3) ....Worked for two years in office occupations.

(Step 4) ....As a clerk-typist for thirteen months, typed a variety of documents including forms, letters, and reports. Also did filing, sorted mail, and answered the telephone.

SAMPLE OF PERFORMANCE INDICATORS

(Step 5) ....Type at 75 w.p.m.

Received two separate merit raises.

Rate of errors in typing was so low that no supervision by employer was needed.

Missed only one day of work in thirteen months.

Was asked to supervise the training of two new employees.

Had better-than-average relationship with all of the supervisory and administrative personnel at my old firm.

PREVIOUS RELATED EXPERIENCE

(Step 6) ....As a keypunch operator for ten months, acquired all the skills involved in keypunching data from a variety of formats.

Was never late for work during the entire time of employment.

Had a better-than-average relationship with 85 percent of my coworkers.

PERSONAL INFORMATION

(Step 8) ....Age: 24

Education: High school graduate

Health: Good

Family status: Married, no children

Note: Since Mary had no particular experience in an area unrelated to the job she wants, she skips step 7 entirely.

57

Table 17. Résumé Based Primarily on Educational Experience

Harry Smith
34 Alden Way
Anywhere, NY 10987
(914) 345-6789

JOB GOAL

Auto Mechanic

SUMMARY OF EDUCATIONAL EXPERIENCE

I have had over 1,200 hours of training in auto repair courses.

As a graduate of Monroe Technical and Vocational High School, I have had over 1,200 hours of training in all phases of auto repair, I can trouble-shoot and repair both mechanical and electrical problems, handle major and minor tune-ups, and deal with routine maintenance jobs such as lubrication and wheel alignment.

I had a B average in auto repair classes, and was in the top 30 percent of all auto repair students.

I am able to use all basic auto repair tools, both manual and power.

SAMPLE OF PERFORMANCE INDICATORS

I was able to learn the basic components of the internal combustion engine faster than 75 percent of my fellow students.

I was never late for any auto class, nor was I ever late in completing an assignment or project.

I had a better-than-average relationship with 80 percent of the students in my auto repair class.

PREVIOUS RELATED EXPERIENCE

As a student-mechanic at Monroe, I helped to organize and run the Car Clinic, a work project that serviced cars owned by both students and faculty.

I started a ''customer recruiting team'' that increased business at the Car Clinic 500 percent during the year I worked there.

I never missed an assignment work session at the Car Clinic.

I have held part-time jobs during the school year and in the summers as an odd-job person and as a lifeguard.

As an odd-job person, I was rehired by the same six families each summer for three years in a row.

I was never absent from my job as a lifeguard.

PERSONAL INFORMATION

Age: 20
Education: High school graduate
Health: Excellent
Family status: Single

Obviously, the rehabilitation practitioner can make modifications of this asset résumé format to suit the individual client's situation. For example, in the résumé illustrated in Table 17, the asset statements begin with the pronoun "I," although the asset statements in the example in Table 16 omit this pronoun.

The eight steps to follow in developing an asset résumé are discussed below.

Step 1: Identifying Self

As indicated in the examples, step 1 is simply a matter of recording the client's full name, full mailing address, and telephone number. This obviously helps the employer to contact the client.

Step 2: Identifying Job Goal

Identifying the job goal means clearly identifying the *type* of job the client is seeking. In helping the client to develop the goal, the practitioner will want to ensure that the goal is neither too broad nor too narrow. If the stated goal is too narrow, the client may miss out on a job for which she/he might otherwise qualify. If the stated goal is too broad, it may be too vague to be of use or may include jobs that the client cannot perform.

Step 3: Highlighting Experience

Step 3 is a brief (one-or-two-sentence) summary of the single experience that best qualifies the client for the position. Usually, this is summarized in terms of time (e.g., number of years worked and/or number of hours of training in the field). This total experience can be taken from the client work and educational forms developed in Chapter 2.

If the client has no significant experience, she/he should use the evidence that indicates most strongly that she/he can do the job.

Step 4: Summarizing Duties and Responsibilities in the Most Important Job-Related Experience

The client's former duties and responsibilities can be taken from the work and educational summary forms. Formats for stating this information are: "As a [position], I [duties and responsibilities]"; or, "As a [position] at [place], I [duties and responsibilities]." The decision to mention the place at which the position was held will depend on whether this will help or hurt the client. If the client learned the skill while in a psychiatric hospital, he/she would certainly not say, "As a trainee in the State Hospital Workshop...". As another example, Mary did not indicate where she was a clerk-typist — at Bradley Insurance — because she planned to apply to a number of noninsurance companies and was afraid this information would hurt her chances.

Remember, the strongest experience goes first. Chronology is irrelevant. The practitioner is helping the clients to show what they have to offer — not when they learned it.

Step 5: Summarizing Assets in the Most Important Job-Related Experience

The résumé next presents, in order of importance, the performance indicators developed in Chapter 2. In general the "can do the job" facts come first, the "dependability" facts second, and the "getting along" facts third. Within each of the three areas, the facts should be listed in the order that will most impress an employer. If the client is applying for a professional position where dependability and punctuality are taken for granted, she/he will need to list only the "can do the job" indicators. However, most clients will be presenting facts from all the areas.

If a potential employer might not understand why a particular fact is important, the client should give the reason (e.g., "I am conscientious, as indicated by the fact that when it was necessary I worked extra hours, at no expense to my employer, to complete assignments given me").

Present the facts in the same format shown in the sample résumés (i.e., in a column no more than four inches wide down the center of the page, with space between each item).

Step 6: Summarizing Experience and Assets in Closely Related Areas

The client may have other experiences that are closely related to the desired job. If so, steps 4 and 5 should be repeated for these other experiences.

Step 7: Summarizing Experience and Assets in Other Relevant Areas

Because the experiences are not closely related, they cannot show directly that the client can do the job. However, this is an opportunity to summarize all other experiences that show that the client is a good worker wherever she/he goes. The format is the same as that used for steps 4 and 5.

Step 8: Supplying Personal Information

In the final step, the client lists those items of personal information that the employer needs to know. These might include the client's age, level of education, family status, and health. Remember, however, that the résumé should include only *positive* information. *The client can wait for a personal interview to present and explain any negative information that the employer needs to know.* If the client dropped out of school, for example, the level of education need not be mentioned in step 8, if this might keep the client from being asked in for an interview.

The law specifically says that an employer cannot hire or refuse to hire anyone on the basis of sex, race, or religion. For this reason, the client need not include information on any of these three areas.

Practice Situations

Based on the directions given above and the two sample résumés shown earlier, practice your own résumé-writing skills by developing a résumé for yourself. Use the asset résumé format illustrated in Table 18. Once this has been completed, work with a client or a friend to develop his/her résumé. Be sure to overview the eight steps and to show an example of a completed résumé. Then, explain each step as you come to it and show the relevant portion of the sample résumé. If possible, the client should do the actual writing so that he/she will feel that the résumé is really his/hers, so that he/she will remember the assets, and so that the practitioner can ensure that the client understands the format.

DEVELOPING A COVER LETTER

If the client is to use the résumé to find unadvertised job openings, she/he will need to develop a cover letter that will serve to introduce the client and to personalize the résumé. Like the résumé, the cover letter is designed to encourage the potential employer to interview the client; and, again like the résumé, eight steps are involved in its development. These are as follows:

Step 1: Addressing the letter

Step 2: Developing a "grabber"

Step 3: Summarizing the strongest experience

Step 4: Identifying the goal

Step 5: Asking for an interview

Step 6: Rounding out the letter

Step 7: Closing and signing

Step 8: Including address

Table 18. Résumé Writing Format

(Step 1).............(self-identification)

_____

_____

_____

_____

JOB GOAL

(Step 2) .... _____

SUMMARY OF EXPERIENCE

(Step 3) ....(strongest qualification)

_____

_____

_____

(Step 4).............(most relevant experience)

_____

_____

_____

SAMPLE OF PERFORMANCE INDICATORS

(Step 5) ....(assets from most relevant experience)

_____

_____

_____

PREVIOUS RELATED EXPERIENCE

(Step 6) ....(assets from related experience)

_____

_____

_____

(Step 7) ....(other experience and assets)

_____

_____

_____

PERSONAL INFORMATION

(Step 8) .... _____

_____

_____

Two sample letters are included in Tables 19 and 20. In Table 19, each of the cover letter steps has been labeled. In Table 20, the steps have been developed but are not labeled, so that the cover letter appears as it might look if it were to be used.

Step 1: Addressing the Letter

In addressing the letter, the client indicates the top person's name and title, the company's name, and the complete address. This information is available from the job list. If the client does not know the top person's name, the title alone would be used.

The client will *not* want to fill in the actual address and salutation until the final copies of this "master" letter are ready for mailing.

Step 2: Developing a "Grabber"

A "grabber" is a statement that captures the interest of the employer by focusing his/her attention on the client's potential value to the employer. This one-sentence opening line can be catchy (e.g., a sales clerk might write, "Let me ring up more profits for you") or straight (e.g., "I want to put my six years of programming experience to work for you"). In general, a catchy phrase is more appropriate for profit-oriented businesses, and a straightforward opener is better for service-oriented organizations.

As a general principle, the grabber should reflect the needs of the employer. In other words, are there any worker characteristics that employers need for this type of position? That is, based on what is known about this job, for what is the person doing the hiring likely to be looking? For example; will he/she be looking for someone who has the energy to work a full eight-hour day with very few breaks? Someone who can work well in noisy conditions? Someone who can wait on tables during a hectic lunch hour and remain calm? Someone who can increase sales? Someone who can handle angry, upset customers? If the client and/or practitioner can identify these employer needs, they can develop a grabber using this information. For example, an applicant for a behind-the-counter waiter position might say: "Why don't you let me help you handle that lunch-hour rush?"

Step 3: Summarizing the Strongest Experience

The client's strongest experience should be summarized briefly in three or four sentences. The summary should describe the duties and responsibilities from the client's most relevant experience and one or two of the strongest performance indicators. This information can be taken from the résumé.

Table 19. Cover Letter Based on Work Experience
(With Steps Identified)

(Date)

(Step 1) ..Ms. Gloria Greenspon, President
Greenspon, Smith, and Paper, Inc.
7890 Larimer Street
Denver, Colorado 80912

Dear Ms. Greenspon:

(Step 2) ...I would like to put my two years of office-work
experience to work for you.

(Step 3) ..As a clerk-typist with a year's experience, I typed
a variety of documents including forms, letters,
and reports. I also did filing, sorted mail, and
answered the phone. I type at 75 w.p.m. My rate of
errors in typing was so low that I needed no
supervision from my employer.

(Step 4) ...I would like to work as an office worker with your
organization.

(Step 5) ...I would like to have a chance to meet with you and
discuss any openings your company might have. I am
available any afternoon after two. I will call you
in the near future to ask about a convenient date for
an interview.

(Step 6) ...Thank you for considering my application.

(Step 7) ....Sincerely,

Mary Jones

(Step 8) ....56 Hilltop Drive
Anytown, Colorado 80990
(303) 987-6789

64

Table 20. Cover Letter Based on Educational Experience

(Date)

Mr. Thomas Taylor, Service Manager
Riverside Garage
56 Thompson Street
Anytown, New York 10546

Dear Mr. Taylor:

I would like a chance to repair cars and raise your profits at
the same time!

I graduated from Monroe Technical where I had over 1,200
hours of training in all phases of auto repair. I can
trouble-shoot and repair mechanical and electrical
problems, perform tune-ups, and handle all routine car
maintenance jobs. I had a B average in my auto repair classes
and was in the top 30 percent of all auto repair students.

I would like to obtain a job at your garage as an auto
mechanic. I can come in at any time for an interview. You can
reach me by mail or by calling me collect at the number
indicated below.

Thank you for your consideration.

Sincerely,

Harry Smith

Harry Smith

34 Alden Way
Anywhere, New York 10987
(914) 345-6789

Step 4: Identifying the Goal

In one sentence, the client lets the employer know what type of job she/he is seeking. The goal is the same as that given in the résumé.

Step 5: Asking for an Interview

In a brief paragraph, the client asks the employer for an interview and indicates when she/he is available. If the client is applying to only a small number of employers, it may be best to indicate that she/he will call the employer rather than wait for a contact. Also, if the client is applying out of town, she/he should indicate that the employer can call collect.

Step 6: Rounding out the Letter

The letter may be rounded out with a line thanking the employer for his/her consideration.

Step 7: Closing and Signing

Step 7 is simply a complimentary closing (e.g., "Sincerely") and the client's signature. The letter should *not* actually be signed until the final copies have been made.

Step 8: Including Address

Beneath the signature, the client should add his/her name as signed, full mailing address, and telephone number. This will ensure that the employer can reach the client.

Practice Situations

As with earlier skills, practice developing a cover letter for yourself first (use the format illustrated in Table 21), and then for a client or a friend. When working with another person, overview each step and show the sample cover letter. Then explain each step as you come to it and show an example. If possible, have the person write his/her own statement.

CONTACTING EMPLOYERS

Once the client has completed his/her résumé and cover letter, each can be readied for use with potential employers. The first step is to have the documents typed.

Table 21. Cover Letter Format

(Date)

Step 1: (Address, taken from job list)

             _____

             _____

             _____

Step 2: (Grabber)

             _____

             _____

             _____

Step 3: (Experience)

             _____

             _____

             _____

Step 4: (Goal)

             _____

             _____

             _____

Step 5: (Interview)

             _____

             _____

             _____

Step 6: (Round out)

             _____

             _____

             _____

                    Step 7: (Close and sign)

                           _____

                           _____

                           _____

                    Step 8: (Address)

                           _____

                           _____

                           _____

The second step is to have the documents copied in sufficient quantity for the client to be able to give one to each potential employer. If copies are made on good "bond" paper, not cheap copy paper, each résumé and letter will look more like an original.

If the client is going to use the résumé and cover letter to contact unadvertised job sources, the date, address, and salutation should be typed on each copy of the letter and the signature added.

FILLING OUT APPLICATIONS

For many jobs, the client will need to fill out a standard application. An accurate, neat, and affective application is another way of presenting oneself in writing. If there are any deficits in this area, the practitioner will want to work with the client on the skills involved. Deficits may be of two major types: (1) the client may not understand a question on the application, or (2) the client may not know how to answer a particular question effectively.

In order to fill out an application, the client will need the following.

1. *A chronological work history:* This should include the dates of employment for each employer (month and year), the employer's address and telephone number, the supervisor's name, the client's starting and ending salary, and the reason for leaving.

2. *A chronological educational history:* This should include the dates the client attended each school, the degrees obtained, and the major courses of study.

3. *Social security number.*

4. *Driver's license.*

5. *A list of three references:* Each reference should include the name, the address, and the telephone number.

Once this information has been gathered, the practitioner can have the client practice filling out application forms. If possible, these should be the actual forms used by some of the companies or organizations to which the client is applying. As the client comes to each question, the practitioner can ask the client how he/she would respond. If the answer is accurate and effective, the client should write it out. If the answer is not accurate or effective, the practitioner will want to give the client an example of what should be said and to explain why this is preferred. The client can then write the answer, while the practitioner ensures that the writing is legible.

The client may have difficulty in answering some questions effectively. One such question is the type that puts the client in a bad light: for example, a "reason for leaving the job" question when the client left because of hospitalization; or a "have you ever been convicted of a nontraffic crime" question when the client is an ex-offender. As a general principle, the client should never just put down a negative fact but, rather, should indicate that she/he would like to talk about it. An alternative would be to use a vague reason that a future interviewer could then ask about. For example, if the client's hospitalization was the reason for leaving, she/he might simply write "illness" or "personal decision." If the client had been fired, she/he might simply write "company decision." Of course, the practitioner would then want to prepare the client to deal with the question in the interview (see the next section of this chapter).

It is also difficult to answer a question when the client does not have sufficient information. The most common question of this type may arise when the employer asks the client what salary she/he wants and the client does not know the salary range offered by that employer. In cases such as these, the client can indicate on the application that the salary is negotiable and can then negotiate with the interviewer after she/he has learned the salary range.

Practice Situations

As a practice exercise, you might obtain some application forms and fill them out yourself. Then work with a client or a friend to collect the needed information and have him/her fill out an application or two. Use the procedure outlined above in order to get practice monitoring and correcting the process.

PRESENTATION OF SELF IN WRITING: A SUMMARY

Goal: To enable the client to obtain an interview with a potential employer.

1. Assist the client in developing a résumé.

2. Assist the client in developing a cover letter.

3. Prepare the résumé and cover letter for use with a potential employer.

4. Identify any deficits the client may have in filling out a standard application form.

PRESENTATION OF SELF IN PERSON

Once the client has done everything possible to contact potential employers, the practitioner will want to help the client to deal with the actual interview. It is unsettling to realize that a very real part of the client's future can depend upon a brief talk with a stranger. Yet this is exactly the nature of the job interview. Although most job interviews last between fifteen minutes and half an hour, studies have shown that interviewers usually decide within the first five minutes whether or not they are really interested in the candidate.

In general, this portion of the chapter is designed to help the practitioner to assist the client in overcoming three main deficits. One deficit involves preparing for the interview in terms of knowing what to wear and what materials to bring. Second type of deficit might be termed "interviewing" deficits — client inadequacies in knowing how to describe themselves to an interviewer in an effective manner. Clients will want to interact with the interviewer in a way that highlights their "can do the job," "dependability," and "getting along" assets. Like the résumé, the goal of the interview is to sell the interviewer on the fact that the client can meet these basic qualifications. The third deficit is in the general area of interpersonal skills — more specifically, inadequacies in the basic courtesy and interaction skills that a client needs to impress an interviewer.

PREPARING FOR THE INTERVIEW

First of all, the client might need to know what to *wear* and what to *bring* to the interview.

In planning with the client what to wear, the practitioner needs one basic guideline: the successful applicant dresses according to what the interviewer will feel is appropriate, and the interviewer usually expects the client to dress like the people already working on that job.

A simple method for preparing the client in this area is to have the client make a list of the things she/he would wear, following up by having the client come to the next session as if dressed for the interview. This will allow for a thorough check of neatness, cleanliness, and appropriateness. If such a dry run is not possible, the practitioner may have the client describe what she/he will wear. The practitioner can then add any comments regarding appropriateness.

The client will also need to know what to bring to the interview. Among the materials necessary for filling out an application, the client will need the chronological work and educational histories and the information on the three references developed earlier. In addition, the client will need a pen, a driver's license, and a social security number. The client will also want to bring his/her résumé (in case the employer does not have one) as well as any special materials related to the desired job (e.g., a draftsman might take a few portfolio drawings).

Finally, by helping the client to explore and answer in writing the following questions, the practitioner can ensure that the client knows how to actually get to the interview.

   1. *Exactly where will the interview be held?* (The client needs to

know not just the street address but the particular building, floor or wing, office number, and so on.)

2. *Who will be interviewing the client?* (It is not always possible to find this out. If the information can be found, however, the client may be able to learn a great deal about what to expect and what will be expected of him/her.)

3. *What is the date and the exact time set for the interview?* (The practitioner should make sure this information is written down.)

4. *Exactly how will the client get to the interview?* (Will he/she drive? Take a bus? A train? Whatever the decision, the practitioner should make sure that there will not be any last-minute foul-ups.)

5. *What exact directions does the client need to know?* (The client must know how to get where he/she is going.)

6. *What time does the client have to leave for the interview?* (The client should plan to leave in plenty of time to get there twenty or thirty minutes early.)

7. *What time does the client need to get up in order to bathe, dress, eat a good breakfast, and still leave at the time given above?*

8. *How should the client use the extra time before the interview?* (The time can best be used for reviewing the materials and checking his/her appearance.)

The practitioner may wish to write each of these questions on a piece of paper to give to the client. The task for the client, then, would be to fill in the answers to these questions before each interview.

JOB-INTERVIEWING SKILLS

Clients will want to be able to describe themselves to the interviewer in positive terms and phrases. The content of job interviews, however, is vastly different from the content that clients are accustomed to in rehabilitation interviews. During rehabilitation interviews, clients are expected and encouraged to talk about the symptoms and their problems. Indeed, some programs accept for services only those clients who are most in need. Thus, clients are indirectly rewarded for presenting themselves in as poor a light as possible.

In the job interview, clients must stress the opposite content; they must describe their strengths rather than their weaknesses. Some psychiatrically disabled clients find this transition difficult. They need to understand the particular tasks involved in a job interview and to be taught how to master these tasks. Although it is true that the psychiatrically disabled person does run a risk of employer discrimination, some research studies suggest that clients who are skilled in job-interviewing techniques can decrease their susceptibility to employer prejudice (Brand and Claiborn, 1976; Farina, Felner, and Boudreau, 1973; Farina and Felner, 1973).

The complexities of a job interview can best be understood by dividing the job-interviewing process into three distinct major tasks: (1) answering the interviewer's questions, (2) asking the interviewer questions, and (3) reviewing the interview. These three tasks correspond roughly to the beginning, middle, and final stages of the job interview. Although each interview is different, the tasks involved in the interview usually occur in the following sequence:

Stage 1: Answering the interviewer's questions

Stage 2: Asking the interviewer questions

Stage 3: Reviewing the interview

Dividing the interviewing process into these three tasks, which occur roughly in this order, makes the process easier for the client to understand and for the practitioner to teach.

During the initial minutes of the interview, the interviewer will undoubtedly ask the client some specific questions. The practitioner will want to prepare the client to answer these questions. The responses here should involve much more than a simple yes or no. The client should learn to do everything possible during this opening phase of the interview to answer the questions by presenting his/her greatest strengths in specific statements and concrete facts. The information used here will almost certainly come from the opening section of the résumé. At the same time, the client must be prepared to answer any "problem" questions that are directed at obvious deficits, such as employment gaps, health, age.

During the middle portion of the interview, the client will need to continue to answer additional questions posed by the interviewer. Here again, the responses should include specific and concrete information about real strengths and capabilities. At the same time, the client should be prepared to ask questions about the position for which he/she is applying. This serves two purposes: (1) it allows the client to gather important information about the job, and (2) it communicates real interest and involvement to the interviewer.

During the brief, final stage of the interview, the client needs to assess the interviewing process by employing a technique called the "hook." This technique allows the client to assess the interview, find out how she/he stands, and correct any problems that may have arisen. In addition, during the final stage, the client must be prepared to use a "call-back" closing, thank the interviewer, and, if necessary, write a follow-up letter.

In essence, clients need to master three sets of skills before an actual interview takes place. They need to know what to *answer*, what to *ask*, and how to *review*. By preparing them to use these skills, the practitioner will have taught the clients how to deal with the interview more skillfully and confidently. Table 22 overviews these three stages.

Table 22. The Three Major Stages of the Job Interview

STAGE 1: *Answering Questions*

> Answering questions so as to highlight greatest strengths
>
> Answering "problem" questions

STAGE 2: *Asking Questions*

> Asking questions to obtain information
> Asking questions to show interest

STAGE 3: *Reviewing the Interview*

> Using the "hook" technique
>
> Using a "call-back" closing
>
> Thanking the interviewer
>
> Writing a letter

Stage 1: Answering the Interviewer's Questions

During the first few minutes of the interview, the client will be responding to specific questions asked by the interviewer. The client will seek to show the interviewer that he/she is the strongest candidate for the job. There are two specific rules of thumb that the practitioner will want to teach clients.

1. ***One of the first responses should be a clear summary of the client's greatest strength.***

    EXAMPLE: Q: *Well, what made you apply to XYZ Company?*

    A: *It seemed like the best move. I have over two hundred hours of training as a _____, and I am anxious to put my skills to work for a company like yours.*

2. ***Monosyllabic, yes or no responses to the interviewer's questions should be avoided.*** The client should not speak excessively but should take every opportunity to present positive information.

    EXAMPLE: Q: *Do you think you would be happy working in fairly close quarters with a number of other people?*

    A: *Definitely. On my last job there were six of us working in a small office, and I got along well with all six people.*

The practitioner will want to teach the clients to present positive *evidence* about themselves and their particular abilities. Table 23 includes eight "typical" interview questions that the client can anticipate. Included are *sample responses* that indicate the way in which such questions can be handled positively by a client. The client can use the knowledge gained from exploring his/her assets (Chapter 2) to help answer many of these questions.

Table 23. Typical Interviewer Questions with Sample Responses

1. *Why do you want to work for us?* Open-ended questions such as these are perfect opportunities for clients to say something positive about themselves or the company. The client should not simply respond that he/she needs a job or is interested in the position. Instead, the client should try to answer in terms of skills and experience and the company's job opportunities. A good response here will show the interviewer that the client has really been thinking about the company. *Sample response: "I feel that your company would be able to put my data-processing skills to use — and would probably give me a chance at promotion if I showed I could do the job!"*

2. *What do you feel are your strengths?* Here the client should obviously mention his/her strongest assets and those strengths that apply most closely to the job at hand. *Sample response: "I think the training I received in auto repairs, both in high school and during my part-time job, is a real strength. In school I kept a high B average in my auto repair classes."*

3. *What are your most important accomplishments?* The client should mention the strongest single fact reflected in the résumé (e.g., grade average, number of promotions or raises, awards or commendations). This fact, however, should be closely related to the job for which the client is being interviewed. *Sample response: "I think my most important achievement was getting my typing speed up to seventy-five words per minute with no decrease in accuracy."*

4. *What other jobs have you held?* If the client has worked in a related area — even if this was not the most recent work experience — he/she can begin with this. If the client has not had much previous experience, this question may be used as a way

74

to get back to other strengths. *Sample response: "I've worked for Zipco for the past three years. By the time I left, I had become the person usually relied on to work on unsupervised jobs."*

5. *What sort of pay are you looking for?* The client will need to learn not to just blurt out an answer to this question — chances are the answer will be either too high or too low. Instead, the client may ask what the range of starting salaries is for someone in the job area and then mention a figure appropriate to her/his past experience. Prior to the interview, the client should have explored the typical pay ranges for this type of position. *Sample response: "Well, can you tell me what secretaries usually start at?"* (Let's say the interviewer cites $3.25 to $4.00 per hour as the starting salary.) *"I'd say that with my training and skill, I'd want to start at around $3.60."*

6. *What have you been earning?* The client can cite the highest pay that she/he has legitimately earned, even if it is not the most recent. If the client is looking for a much higher wage than previously earned, specific assets can be cited as reasons for the company to pay this higher wage. *Sample response: "I earned a hundred and twenty-five dollars a week as a sales clerk. But that was before I finished my training program at night school. I feel that my new skills in accounting qualify me for higher pay."*

7. *When can you start?* The client can get a range of possible starting dates from the interviewer and give a date that falls within that range. *Sample response: "You want someone by the first of May, is that right? Well, I do have some other interviews. But if you decide you're interested in me and I decide I'm equally interested, I could certainly begin work before that date — say, by April fifteenth."*

8. *What are your future plans?* (The interviewer wants to know whether the applicant's plans and the company's are compatible.) The client may answer in terms of the type of work that might be done for this company in the future. *Sample response: "I certainly hope to become a foreman."*

Besides being able to answer questions that allow the client to describe assets, the client will also need to be able to answer questions directed at deficits. For instance, the interviewer may ask some variation of the questions: "What about [deficit]? Is [deficit] going to present any problems?" The interviewer is focusing on what may seem a specific client weakness, such as employment history, the fact that the client is younger or older than the typical age for the job, previous disability, over- or under-qualification, or present employment status. The client can respond to these questions in a positive manner without concealment, apologies, or unnecessary detail.

The practitioner can teach the client a two-step process for toning down deficits. First, the client can learn to rephrase the deficit by using everyday language, avoiding uncomplimentary labels (e.g., high school dropout), and stating the deficit as positively as possible. For example, the deficit of *"mental patient"* can be rephrased to *"I sought help for some emotional problems"*; the deficit of *"unemployed for one-half year"* can be rephrased to *"I have been looking for the right job for me for about six months"*; the deficit of *"high school dropout"* can be rephrased to *"I decided to leave high school during my senior year."*

Once the practitioner and client have rephrased the deficit, the second step is to overcome it by using one of three strategies.

The deficit may be turned into an asset: *"I did seek help for some emotional problems, and I received excellent help. Because of that help, I am probably in as good or better shape than almost any other applicant you will see."*

The deficit may be compensated for by showing how other characteristics help alleviate it: *"Although I do learn a little more slowly than other people, I don't get bored as easily with a routine task."*

The client may deny that the deficit is critical: *"Although this is my first full-time experience as a dental assistant, in my practical experiences at school I was always rated very highly."*

Thus, the client can be prepared to discuss any deficits that the employment interviewer already knows, can easily observe, or will probably find out about. Other areas of the client's life in which he/she might be having difficulty (e.g., marriage, child-rearing) need not be mentioned. The client needs to learn that the job interview, unlike a rehabilitation interview, is not the setting in which to be completely revealing.

Stage 2: Asking the Interviewer Questions

This phase is essentially a continuation of the earlier phase; the client continues to answer questions by mentioning assets. At the same time, however, the client can learn to show interest and obtain information by asking some questions of his/her own that are *related* to the content of the interview. For example, if the interviewer asks, *"How do you feel about working overtime?"* a client answer that closes with a question might be: *"I've never been afraid of work at any time. On my last job, I came in on the average of one Saturday a month to finish up jobs left undone by other employees. This didn't involve any extra pay, since I was paid a salary rather than an hourly wage. Maybe you can tell me a little bit about what you expect of employees in the _____ department in terms of overtime?"*

Besides being prepared to ask questions relevant to any information the client might need, the client can also learn to ask questions that show him/her as a worker who is interested in the job. The following are some typical questions that clients might learn to ask.

1. *As a _____ , what would my particular duties and responsibilities be?*

2. *In general, what does _____ Company expect from new employees hired in this job area?*

3. *Is there anything in the way of particular materials or equipment that I would need before I started work?*

The client will not want to ask about such sensitive subjects as pay, fringe benefits, or promotions until one of two things has happened: (1) the interviewer has brought up these subjects, and the client can therefore frame the question as a response; or (2) the interviewer has made the client a definite offer of a job. Once either of these things has happened, the client can initiate by asking about pay, company fringe benefits, and the chances for promotion.

Stage 3: Reviewing the Interview

Having answered all the interviewer's questions and asked his/her own questions, the client will want to know where she/he stands in relation to obtaining the job. For those instances where no job offer is made immediately, the client can use a questioning technique to get a clear idea of where she/he stands: this technique is called the *"hook."*

The hook is simply a single question that the client can pose to the interviewer. In typical form, the hook might go something like this: *"Well, I've tried to answer your questions by giving you some details about my own background and experience. Are there any areas where you still have some questions about me?"*

In using the hook, the client is taking control of the interview. If the interviewer has already decided that the client is a prime candidate for the job, the initiative shown here will strengthen the chances. If the interviewer has decided for some reason that the client is *not* the best candidate, the use of the hook may help the client discover what the interviewer sees as weakness. In other words, the interviewer is being given a chance to express any doubts or questions about the applicant. If the interviewer expresses no doubts, the client can reflect his/her understanding by responding with a format such as *"You're saying _____."* (Example: *"So you're saying that you're satisfied with what I've presented.")*

If the interviewer *does* express specific doubts, the client can ob-

77

viously respond to these doubts with some additional positive information. In either event, the client will receive more information about how the interview was perceived by the interviewer.

An interview is usually concluded with the interviewer telling the client that the company *"will be in touch very soon,"* or that *"as soon as we make a decision, we will give you a call."* Many applicants are willing to end the interview on this note. However, it is more effective to terminate the interview by using a "call-back" closing. The practitioner can teach the client to indicate that the client will get in touch with the interviewer if she/he does not hear within a certain period of time. For example, *"I have some other appointments this week, so I may not be at home when you call. I'm really very interested in the job. If it's all right with you, I will give you a call within several days to find out what you've decided."*

The call-back closing not only reaffirms the client's interest in the job but also allows the client to keep her/his foot in the door. The call-back phone call will serve to remind the employer of the interview. Also, if the interviewer decides not to hire the client, the client may be told why and can use this information to improve her/his interviewing skills.

Finally, the practitioner will want to teach the client to remember to thank the interviewer for his/her time. The client should also learn to thank the receptionist, since interviewers so often ask their receptionists for their impressions of applicants. Once the interview is over, the client may also wish to write a brief note as a follow-up. Below is a sample.

If a note is written, it is extremely important that it *be written and sent on the same day as the interview,* so that the interviewer will receive the note only a day or two later and will be reminded of the client's interest and enthusiasm.

Dear Mr./Mrs./Miss/Ms. (last name):

Thank you very much indeed for taking the time to meet with me and discuss the position as (name of position for which client applied).

I am still extremely interested in this position. Please do let me know as soon as you have reached a decision on my application.

Thank you again.

Sincerely,

(Signature)

(Name)
(Address)
(Telephone)

Interpersonal Skills in the Job Interview

In addition to the substantive information on handling an interview given above, there are interpersonal aspects of successful interviewing. The necessary interpersonal skills can be summarized in ten basic *"commandments."*

1. *Don't* take anyone with you to the interview. The employer wants to see you, not your friends!

2. *Don't* chew gum or smoke during the interview. It is possible that the interviewer may smoke. He or she will not necessarily respect an applicant who shares his vice, however.

3. *Don't* lounge back in your chair as though you were at home. This gives the interviewer an impression of carelessness.

4. *Don't* mumble or speak in a low, hard-to-hear voice. The interviewer doesn't want to *work* to hear what you're saying.

5. *Don't* pepper your statements with slang expressions or meaningless rhetoric such as "y'know." The interviewer is interested in, among other things, how well you can present yourself verbally.

6. *Do* introduce yourself to the receptionist. Give your name, the name of the person you are there to see, and the time of your appointment with that person.

7. *Do* greet the interviewer politely, looking him/her in the eye while mentioning your name clearly and giving him or her a firm handshake.

8. *Do* sit forward in your chair, leaning slightly in toward the interviewer to let him or her know that you are attending carefully.

9. *Do* make frequent eye contact with the interviewer. Again, this lets the interviewer know that you are attending with interest.

10. *Do* speak clearly, distinctly, and to the point. In this way, you can help the interviewer feel that the two of you are really communicating.

Practice Situations

There are two things you can do to assist clients in handling job interviews. First, answer the common interviewer questions for yourself. Then, practice by taking a friend or a client through the entire procedure of preparing for and handling the interview. After he/she has developed all the content answers, it is critical that you practice simulating an interview. This will ensure that your clients receive the behavior rehearsal opportunity needed to put the interpersonal skills and interviewing content together.

The clients will learn the skills of interviewing most effectively if the practitioner takes them through an explain-demonstrate-practice teaching process for each particular skill. (This skill-teaching process is discussed in detail in Book 2, *The Skills of Rehabilitation Programming*.) In essence, the practitioner *explains* to the client what is involved in each skill step, *demonstrates* how the skill is performed, and then provides the client with opportunities to *practice* the skill. These practice sessions may occur in a variety of simulated situations and may concentrate on one interviewing phase at a time. The final practice situation should approximate the real interviewing situation as closely as is possible.

As the client begins to conduct interviews with employers, the practitioner will want to monitor and support the client's performance. If the client becomes discouraged by a lack of initial success, the practitioner will want to be interpersonally supportive to the client. Also, the practitioner might want to modify and/or practice those aspects of the interviewing process that are still difficult for the client.

PRESENTATION OF SELF IN PERSON: A SUMMARY

Goal: To help the client to deal effectively with the actual interview.

1. Prepare the client for the interview. Make sure the client will be dressed appropriately, will bring the necessary materials and information, and knows how to get to the interview.

2. Prepare the client for the content of the interview. Prepare the client to answer questions, ask questions, and review the interview.

3. Make sure the client understands the important interpersonal aspects of the interview.

4. Monitor and support the client's interviewing experience.

ACTING TO PRESENT SELF: A SKILLED APPROACH

"I don't know ..." Bonita shook her head. "I mean, it was one thing just filling out the applications and everything. None of the questions on the applications asked me why I had been out of work — out of everything — almost all this year. But now I'm starting to get these interviews. And the people who talk to me, they can ask anything they like, and I've got to come up with a good answer. So — so what happens if they ask me about being unemployed? What if they find out I've been in the hospital?"

Ken leaned forward and caught her eyes with his own. "Right now you're pretty scared because you don't have any way to deal with questions about your hospitalization," he said. "But that's exactly the kind of thing I can help you with. And I'll tell you how we're going to start."

Bonita's first interview for a secretarial job took place the next week. The firm to which she had applied, Hubbard, Crouse, and Walters, Inc., was a highly respectable insurance agency. Their offices on the third floor of an older midtown building were paneled in dark wood and richly carpeted. The subdued, almost reverential hush that lay over the rooms extended to the prim receptionist who asked Bonita's name and business in softly rounded syllables. Bonita supplied the information requested, and the receptionist disappeared through a heavy door, closing it silently behind her.

Sammi told me that HCW pays top dollar, Bonita thought as she surveyed her surroundings. I guess he wasn't kidding!

When the receptionist reappeared and beckoned her, Bonita marveled at her own relative composure. Oh, she was nervous, all right — who wouldn't be? But the paralyzing fear that had gripped her the day before seemed strangely absent. The plan she had worked out with Ken helped — it helped a lot!

The man who interviewed Bonita, a Mr. Henry, had obviously read between the lines of her application. After asking a few initial questions about her background, he brought up the subject of Bonita's recent unemployment.

"Well, what happened was that I had some personal concerns that needed to be worked out," Bonita told him. "The fact is, I spent about three months in the hospital. Since then, I've been working on a regular basis with one of the counselors there. Both my doctor and my counselor feel that I'm in excellent shape now — better than before, really."

Now came what Bonita and Ken had agreed was one of the most important parts: "You see, my past employers always said good things about my secretarial skills. I can type seventy words per minute, almost always error free. My shorthand is up over a hundred and ten words a minute. But before I decided to go into the hospital, I sometimes had trouble keeping myself organized. Now I've learned how to handle that end of things really well. In fact, during the three months I've been getting counseling on an outpatient basis, I've been able to take over the accounts for the store my parents run — that's something I could never have done before!"

Bonita saw that Mr. Henry's initial expression of concern was changing into something resembling respectful interest. She wasted no time driving her point home. "I know that to you my hospitalization may make me seem like a bit of a risk. But I think if you read the letters I brought with me from my counselor and past employers you'll see my skills and motivation really make me more than a safe bet — they show I can do exactly the job that your company wants done."

Bonita was finished. In truth, it was clear that she had more than answered Mr. Henry's question. The man who sat across from her was clearly impressed. What's more, he as much as said so.

"Thank you, Bonita. I think you've told me everything I wanted to know. And I think — no, I'm sure — that I'll be able to give you some good news about your application as soon as I've firmed a few things up about pay and so on with our personnel people."

The excitement Bonita felt was by no means a private affair. Beneath everything else, she felt a deep sense of gratitude to Ken. Without his help, she could never have managed things this well. But with such help — well, it seemed as though the sky was the limit!

Chapter 5 APPLICATIONS IN EDUCATION AND TRAINING

To this point, this text has focused on helping psychiatric rehabilitation clients to place themselves in a job. The need for job placement is one practitioners will often face with their clients. At times, however, the practitioner will be working with a client who desires placement in an educational or training setting. For example, the client may desire placement in a four- year college, a two-year college, a CETA job opening, an apprenticeship, or some other paid, trainee position.

The client deficits that would indicate a need for placement skills in regard to getting a position as a student or trainee are the same as those cited in Chapter 1. In particular, clients may find they (1) cannot identify the assets that qualify them for the trainee position and/or (2) cannot identify potential sources of training and/or (3) cannot present themselves in writing (applications and résumés) and/or (4) cannot present themselves in an interview because of interpersonal or interviewing deficits.

The focus of the present chapter, then, will be to review the skills developed in earlier chapters in light of any changes relevant to making educational/training applications.

EXPLORING ASSETS

SUMMARIZING PAST WORK EXPERIENCE

Summarizing past work experience for educational/training purposes involves no real process changes. A chronological work history is developed, and the job or jobs that relate to the desired training position are checked off. If none of the work experiences is especially relevant, the practitioner can work with the client to identify the job that he/she performed best or the one in which the client demonstrated the most learning ability. When detailing the duties and responsibilities of the jobs, the practitioner will want to help the client to emphasize what she/he learned to do there. This can be done by simply having the client indicate the duties performed on that job.

SUMMARIZING PAST EDUCATIONAL EXPERIENCE

The process described previously to summarize educational experience will be used again. Here practitioner and client explore previous educational experiences and the details of those that are most relevant.

Usually, the most recent educational experience will be the most relevant. If the client desires training in a two- or four-year school, the high school transcript may play a vital role. In this case, the practitioner may want to have the client secure a copy of the transcript to serve as a stimulus for summarizing details of what was learned and selecting the indicators of performance.

IDENTIFYING ASSETS FROM WORK EXPERIENCE

The client will still want to use concrete facts (i.e., numbers, percentages, absolute words, and specific amounts) in identifying assets. He/she will still want to use the same concrete and comparative questions. (How much did I do? How did that compare to others? How well did I do? How did that compare?) Although many of the assets can be used to show that the client performs tasks well, is dependable, and gets along with coworkers, the practitioner will want to pay special attention here to the "speed of learning" indicators.

IDENTIFYING ASSETS FROM EDUCATIONAL EXPERIENCE

Grade achievement will obviously be the most critical factor in identifying assets from educational experience. This will be particularly true for clients aspiring to two- and four-year colleges. The practitioner will want to make every effort to identify positive indicators of performance. As noted earlier, a transcript may help to stimulate a complete exploration of the client's achievements.

UNDERSTANDING EDUCATIONAL/TRAINING OPPORTUNITIES

DETERMINING GEOGRAPHIC LOCATION

As before, the practitioner will want to help the client to identify the geographic location within which she/he will seek a training position. As with job seeking, the clients need to decide where they will live, whether they are willing to relocate, and what their travel and transportation limitations are.

ACTING TO OBTAIN AN EDUCATIONAL/TRAINING POSITION

WRITING THE RÉSUMÉ

The format to be used in developing the résumé for an educational/training position is identical to that used earlier for jobs. However, there are some minor variations in content. In terms of step 2 (identifying the goal), the same principle applies; the goal should be stated broadly enough to incorporate all desired positions, yet narrowly enough to eliminate unwanted or unattainable positions. Thus, if the educational/training setting offers more than one program, the client will need to decide whether she/he is applying for just any position (i.e., student or trainee) or for a specific position (e.g., welding student or licensed-practical-nurse student).

Step 3 (highlighting experience) remains unchanged. As before, clients can summarize the amount of related training they have had and/or the amount of time spent working in a related field. If the client does not have a significant amount of relevant training or experience but is still qualified for entry, step 3 may be omitted. Step 4 (summarizing the most relevant experience) is also unchanged. Where the most relevant experience is a job, the client may want to indicate how much she/he learned as part of the experience (e.g., "As a department store clerk, I learned to wait on customers; to record cash, check, and credit transactions; to take and maintain inventory; and to handle mail and telephone orders").

Step 5 (summarizing the client's assets in the most relevant experience) involves the same procedures that were used previously. As has been suggested, if the most relevant experience is a job, the practitioner may want to help the client to emphasize the performance indicators that concern his/her ability to learn. When applying for a position in a traditional and/or professional educational/training setting, the client will want to emphasize performance assets and deemphasize the assets of dependability and getting along with coworkers.

Steps 6 to 8 (summarizing other expeiences and supplying personal information) remain unchanged and may be completed as they were on the job résumé.

WRITING A COVER LETTER

In applying for an educational/training position, the applicant will need to make some revisions in the format of the cover letter. Basically, step 2 (the grabber) is deleted; there is no need to grab the readers' attention by emphasizing what the client can do for them. Thus, the steps in this case are as follows:

Step 1:   Addressing the letter

Step 2:   Identifying the goal

Step 3:   Summarizing the strongest experience

Step 4:   Asking for an interview

Step 5:   Rounding out the letter

Step 6:   Closing and signing

Step 7:   Including address

Although the format of the letter changes, the content of the individual steps remains exactly the same as in the job-application cover letter.

CONTACTING EDUCATIONAL/TRAINING ORGANIZATIONS

The procedures for finalizing and reproducing the application documents and contacting the educational/training institutions are the same as those described earlier for clients seeking job placement.

FILLING OUT APPLICATIONS

As with job applications, the practitioner will need to make sure that clients (1) know what is needed to fill out an application (including the chronological work and educational histories), (2) are able to understand the questions that are asked on applications at the types of places to which they are applying, and (3) know how to answer questions that concern their deficits. The procedures for helping clients with these tasks have been presented in the job-application section of this text.

INTERVIEWING

In preparing for the interview, clients will need to bring the same things, follow the same principles of dress, and make the same specific plans that were described earlier in the job-interviewing section. In terms of handling the interview, clients will want to be prepared to handle exactly the same questions, with the exception of salary and starting-date questions. The stages of the interview (i.e., answering, asking, and reviewing) remain the same. The ten interpersonal commandments for interviewees also apply. In short, interviewing for an educational/training position is very similar to interviewing for a job — which means that it must be approached by practitioner and client alike in a careful and painstaking manner.

IDENTIFYING SOURCES OF INFORMATION ABOUT OPPORTUNITIES

The distinction between advertised and unadvertised openings that was used in relation to job seeking does not apply in regard to training opportunities. Therefore, these steps are collapsed when helping a client to identify possible sources of education or training. Sources of information about possible training opportunities include:

1. General handbooks about colleges
2. Individual college catalogues
3. Yellow Pages (under "Schools")
4. State Employment Security Division (apprenticeships and CETA programs)
5. Labor and professional organizations
6. School counseling offices
7. Rehabilitation agencies
8. State Department of Education
9. City Hall (CETA and other manpower programs)
10. Local office, U.S. Department of Labor (apprenticeship programs)

As suggested in Chapter 3, the above are general sources of information about possible training opportunities; the practitioner will want to help the client to identify the specific sources to be used. This will mean answering the following questions.

1. *What* is the name of the source?
2. *Where* is it located?
3. *Whom* do you contact to obtain the information or the written source?
4. *How* do you contact them?
5. *How* do you use the source to get the needed information?

Once the specific sources of information about possible openings have been identified, they can be used to compile a list of places to apply for training.

DEVELOPING THE EDUCATIONAL/TRAINING OPPORTUNITIES LIST

The educational/training opportunity list is similar to the list developed for jobs. It should contain the following information:

1. Organization name and address (including the ZIP code)

2. Name and title of the person to whom the application will be sent (admissions officer if the source is a school, director if the source is a program, top administrator if the source is an employer)

3. Telephone number

Practice Situations

As a first practice step, you will want to work on your own to develop a list of twenty-five to fifty educational/training opportunities, either for training in which you would be interested or for training in which many of your clients would be interested. Then, work with a client or a friend to practice developing a list of opportunities for him or her. As you did earlier, try to select someone to whom you can teach the use of the various sources so that you can get practice in this aspect of the delivery.

Remember to follow the explain-demonstrate-practice procedure that has been used throughout this manual.

Chapter 6 AN OVERVIEW OF CAREER PLACEMENT SKILLS

EVALUATING THE EFFECTIVENESS OF CAREER PLACEMENT

OUTCOME MEASURES

A number of outcome measures can be used to assess the effectiveness of career placement. Each of these is discussed below.

Placement

Placement, of course, is the most basic outcome measure. Either the placement process results in the client's obtaining a position as an employee or as a student/trainee or it does not. The number of interviews generated can also be used as an interim measure of placement.

Efficiency of the Placement

There are several indicators of the efficiency of the placement. One of these is *time*. That is, how long did it take the client to acquire a position? The point from which the length of time is measured can be the initial client contact date or the date on which the client began contacting employers. A second measure of placement efficiency can be the *ratio of offers to interviews*. That is, how frequently is the client offered a job when she/he has an interview?

Effectiveness of the Placement

As before, several measures of placement effectiveness can be used. Perhaps the best and most critical measure is *position retention*. If the client enrolls in an educational/training position, does he/she complete it? If the client obtains a job, how long does she/he remain in it?

A second measure of placement effectiveness is general client *satisfaction*. For example, the practitioner may simply ask the client how satisfied she/he is with the position on a scale of 1 to 10, where 1 is not satisfied at all and 10 is totally satisfied.

A third possible measure of placement effectiveness is the degree to which the position fits the client's previously identified *interests, abilities, and educational achievement.*Occupations can be divided into seven basic interest areas:

Data Occupations. These occupations stress working almost exclusively with data. The data can be in the form of words or numbers. There is very limited emphasis on interacting with people. If equipment is used at all, it is used simply as a means to process data. Examples in this area would include typists, meter readers, bookkeepers, computer programmers, accountants, and economists.

People Occupations. These occupations stress working almost exclusively with people, usually in a service or helping role. The worker uses little or no equipment or information in his/her work. Examples in this area would include waiters/waitresses, security officers, service station attendants, models, and flight attendants.

Things Occupations. These occupations stress working almost exclusively with tools and equipment. Little or no interaction with people is required. Few data are used in performing the job. Examples in this area include factory assemblers, long-distance truck drivers, welders, heavy-machinery operators, and meat cutters.

Data/People Occupations. These occupations require working with both people and data. Use of equipment is not central to performing the job. Examples from this area include telephone operators, receptionists, travel agents, department store or general salespersons, policemen, teachers, and counselors.

Data/Things Occupations. These occupations require working with both written or numerical information and tools and equipment. Interacting with other people is only a minimal job requirement. Examples from this area include various types of mechanics, carpenters, electricians, bricklayers, repair persons, dental technicians, engineers, chemists, and biologists.

People/Things Occupations. These occupations require working with both people and things. Determining or using information is minimal. Examples here would include orderlies, nurse's aides, home attendants, veterinary assistants, and recreation leaders.

Data/People/Things Occupations. These occupations require working with people, information, and tools and equipment as part of the job. Examples from this area would include cooks, photographers, automobile and parts salespersons, barbers and beauticians, dental hygienists, veterinarians, physicians, and nurses.

Initially, the practitioner can have the client rank the different categories from most preferred (7) to least preferred (1). Any position can then be categorized into one of the groups. A deviation score from the preferred interest area can eventually be obtained by subtracting the category rank in which the actual position fits from the most preferred category. Thus, if the category in which the actual position fits is ranked 6, then the deviation score would be 1 (most preferred category = 7; actual position's category = 6; 7 – 6 = 1).

This process can be repeated in terms of education. In other words, does the actual position make use of the client's past educational achievement? Educational achievement can be categorized at five different levels as follows:

Educational Level 5. Occupations in this category require four years of college or graduate school training. Examples of occupations in this category include various types of scientists, teachers, registered nurses, doctors, and engineers.

Educational Level 4. Occupations in this category require two years of junior or community college training, or three to four years of apprenticeship. Examples of occupations in this category include computer programmers, law enforcement officers, restaurant and hotel/motel management, medical and legal secretaries, insurance agents, dental and x-ray technicians, carpenters and construction electricians, flight attendants, and recreation supervisors.

Educational Level 3. Occupations in this category require from six to twenty-three months of technical vocational school or apprenticeship training after high school. Examples of occupations in this category include bookkeepers, clerk-typists, bank tellers, long-distance operators, secretaries, various types of mechanics (e.g., air conditioning, diesel, refrigeration), draftsmen, heavy-equipment operators, and meat cutters.

Educational Level 2. Occupations in this category require a high school diploma or its equivalent and up to five months of training. Examples of occupations in this area include typists, meter readers, food store clerks, various retail salespersons, insurance claims clerks, receptionists, local truck drivers, mail carriers, and nurse's aides or orderlies.

Educational Level 1. Occupations in this category do not require a high school diploma or its equivalent. Examples of occupations in this category include bartenders, waiters/waitresses, short-order cooks, stock clerks, service station attendants, factory assemblers, laborers, and janitors.

A deviation score can be obtained by taking the client's level of education and subtracting from it the level of education required by the positions. For example, if the client was a high school graduate and the actual position attained did not require high school, there would be a score of 1 (high school graduate = 2; actual position = 1; 2–1 = 1).

The sum of the interest deviation score and the educational deviation score can indicate the quality of the "fit" between the client and the position.

A fourth potential indicator of the effectiveness of a placement is the salary of the position. In particular, one can compare the salary difference between the obtained job and the client's previous job or jobs. It is usually best to compare the present salary with the salary of the client's last job and/or the client's highest paid job.

As evidenced above, all outcome measures may not be equally applicable to a particular case. By the same token, these measures are by no means mutually exclusive. In addition, different measures can be used at different times. Because job-retention evaluation clearly takes time, client satisfaction may be used as an interim measure. Thus, the practitioner can select from among the outcome measures those which are most appropriate for evaluating a particular client at a particular point in time.

PROCESS MEASURES

Process measures refer to evaluation of the effectiveness of the placement process rather than placement outcome. In particular, the skills and knowledge relevant to placement can be evaluated. At the simplest level, the placement process can be evaluated by determining (1) whether or not the client has a résumé that at least contains his/her address, highlight of experience, goal, summary of the most relevant experience, factual indicators of performance from that experience, and positive personal information; and (2) whether or not the client has a list of twenty-five or more potential employers or has identified resources that can refer him/her to at least half a dozen employers for an interview.

At the next level, the client's skills can be assessed. In particular, the evaluation should focus on: *(a)* the client's ability to identify his/her assets; *(b)* the client's ability to identify advertised and unadvertised job openings; *(c)* the client's ability to present self in writing (e.g., résumé and application); *(d)* the client's ability to present self in person (e.g., answering typical interviewer questions).

Table 24 lists sample skills questions that can be used, in whole or in part, to identify the client's skill level. Although any question can be modified to fit a particular client and/or other questions can be added, it should be noted that skills questionnaires actually ask the client to perform the skill. Thus, the client will need to be able to *use* the skill, not simply to write about it. A skills questionnaire can be used not only to find out what the client knows after counseling but also as a precounseling diagnostic test. Discrepancies between pre- and post-scores can also be used to obtain a more accurate picture of skill gains.

It should be noted that the interviewer questions may also be administered orally. However, this makes scoring more difficult; the score could be depressed by client anxiety, particularly in the prediagnostic phase. This last consideration must be weighed in terms of these disadvantages versus the client's ability to write.

The use of the skills inventory is most important during the early stages of practitioner delivery of these placement skills to clients. By using the instrument, at least in the postcounseling process, the practitioner can evaluate the degree to which he/she is getting the skills across to the clients. Finally, it should be noted that these same skills questions can also be used to evaluate the level of functioning of any practitioner whose job it is to prepare clients for placement.

CONDUCTING A CAREER PLACEMENT DIAGNOSIS

A practitioner who has mastered all the career placement skills is in a position to make a comprehensive diagnosis of a client's skills in order to determine what career placement skills the client has, as well as what career placement skills the client will need to develop to pursue a specific career objective. Obviously, if the career objective is such that the rehabilitation practitioner does the placement for the client (e.g., hospital-based sheltered workshop), the client does not need his/her placement skills diagnosed. However, if the short- or long-term objective includes competitive employment, then a comprehensive diagnosis of the client's career placement skills would be in order.

As mentioned previously, the career-placement-skills questions (Table 24) can form the basis of a career placement diagnosis. By using these or similar questions, the practitioner can assess exactly what the client needs in terms of career placement skills. After the diagnosis is complete, the practitioner can then either make a detailed referral to some other appropriate practitioner or begin to teach the client the needed skills.

Table 24. Placement Skills Questionnaire

I. Ability to Identify Assets

Please list below the things you could tell a potential employer about yourself to show that you

(a) can do the job;
(b) are a dependable worker;
(c) get along with others.

Notes: 1. Leave enough space between items *a, b,* and *c* for the client to write.

2. Assess by making sure the client has at least three specific facts (i.e., statements that include a number, percentage, absolute word, amount, performance indicator, or comparative word).

II. Ability to Develop Potential Job Positions

A. Please list below whom you could talk to or what you could read to find out where there are job openings for the position you desire.

B. Please list below the *general types* of employers or companies that hire employees for the type of position you desire.

Note: Assess by looking at the number of places or people the client can list as being either *(a)* helpful on his/her job search or *(b)* potential employers.

III. Ability to Present Self in Writing

A. *Résumé writing:* Develop a written summary of your experience (résumé) that you could send or give to a potential employer.

Notes: 1. Leave a whole page for this item.

2. Assess by checking whether the client has included address, telephone number, highlighted experience, goal, summary of most relevant experience, at least three factual assets from that experience, and positive personal information.

B. *Filling out applications:* Please fill out the accompanying application.

Notes: 1. Include an application from an employer appropriate to the client.

2. Assess by making sure the client has
(a) answered all questions accurately;
(b) not presented any deficits in writing;
(c) written all items clearly and legibly.

94

IV. **Ability to Present Self in Person**

A. *Answering questions:* Imagine that each of the following questions has been asked of you in an interview. Write down exactly what you would say to the interviewer. (If assessment is administered orally, say exactly what you would say to the interviewer.)

1. Why do you want to work for us? (Assess client's ability to link her/his assets to opportunities offered by the company.)

2. What do you feel are your strengths? (Assess client's ability to list at least one factual performance indicator.)

3. What other experiences have you had? (Assess client's ability to give a summary of duties and responsibilities and at least one factual asset.)

4. What other jobs have you held? (Assess client's ability to use this question as a way to talk about his/her strengths.)

5. What are your most important accomplishments? (Assess client's ability to give at least one factual asset.)

6. What sort of pay are you looking for? (Assess client's ability to solicit input about the wage range.)

7. What have you been earning? (Assess client's ability to show that her/his assets deserve that pay.)

8. When can you start? (Assess client's ability to solicit input about the range of starting dates.)

9. What are your future plans? (Assess client's ability to link his/her plans to opportunities offered by the employer.)

10. What about [deficit]? (If possible, individualize the deficit for the client. If this is not possible, pick a deficit that will fit most clients—e.g., unemployment or age. Assess the client's ability to use a strategy to overcome the deficit.)

B. *Asking questions:* Write (or say) those questions that you would ask an interviewer. (Assess the client's ability to ask information questions and "showing interest" questions. Is the client's first question about pay or fringe benefits?)

C. *Reviewing the interview:* Write (or say) what you would say or do near the end of the interview. (Assess the client's ability to use the "hook" technique and the "call-back" closing, as well as whether the client remembers to thank the interviewer.)

REFERENCES

Anderson, J. A.   The disadvantaged seek work—through their efforts or ours? *Rehabilitation Record,* 1968, *9,* 5-10.

Anthony, W. A.   *Principles of psychiatric rehabilitation.* Amherst, MA: Human Resource Development Press, 1979.

Anthony, W. A.; Buell, G. J.; Sharratt, S.; and Atthoff, M. E.   The efficacy of psychiatric rehabilitation. *Psychological Bulletin,* 1972, *78,* 447-456.

Anthony, W. A.; Cohen, R. M.; and Vitalo, R.   The measurement of rehabilitation outcome. *Schizophrenia Bulletin,* 1978, *4,* 365-383.

Bean, B. R., and Beard, J. H.   Placement for persons with psychiatric disability. *Rehabilitation Counseling Bulletin,* 1975, June, 253-258.

Brand, R. C., and Claiborn, W. L.   Two studies of comparative stigma: Employer attitudes and practices toward rehabilitated convicts, mental and tuberculosis patients. *Community Mental Health Journal,* 1976, *12,* 168-175.

Cannon, J. R., and Pierce, R. M.   Order effects in the experimental manipulation of therapeutic conditions. *Journal of Clinical Psychology,* 1968, *24,* 242-244.

Farina, A., and Felner, R.   Employment interviewer reactions to former mental patients. *Journal of Abnormal Psychology,* 1973, *82,* 268-272.

Farina, A.; Felmer, R.; and Boudreau, L.   Reactions of workers to male and female mental patient job applicants. *Journal of Consulting and Clinical Psychology,* 1973, *41,* 363-372.

Keil, E. L., and Barbee, J. R.   Behavior modification and training the disadvantaged job interviewee. *Vocational Guidance Quarterly,* 1973, September, 50-56.

Keith, R. D.; Engelkes, J. R.; and Winborn, B. B.   Employment-seeking preparation and activity: An experimental job-placement training model for rehabilitation clients. *Rehabilitation Counseling Bulletin,* 1977, December, 159-165.

Levitan, S. A., and Taggert, R.   *Jobs for the disabled.* Baltimore: Johns Hopkins University Press, 1977.

McClure, D. P.   Placement through improvement of client's job seeking skills. *Journal of Applied Rehabilitation Counseling,* 1973, *3,* 188-196.

Prazak, J. A.   Learning job seeking interview skills. In Krumboltz and Thoreson (Eds.), *Behavioral Counseling,* pp. 414-424. New York: Holt, Rinehart & Winston, 1969.

Pumo, B.; Sehl, R.; and Cogan, F.   Job readiness: Key to placement. *Journal of Rehabilitation,* 1966, *32,* 18-19.

Safieri, D.   Using an education model in a sheltered workshop program. *Mental Hygiene,* 1970, *54,* 140-143.

Truax, C. B., and Carkhuff, R. R.   *Toward effective counseling and psychotherapy.* Chicago, IL: Aldine, 1967.

Zadny, J. J., and James, L. F.   Another view on placement: State of the art—1976. *Studies in Placement: Monograph No. 1.* Portland State University, Portland, OR.